A Guide to Prehistoric Sites in Herefordshire

Monuments in the Landscape

Volume I

A Guide to Prehistoric Sites in Herefordshire

by
George Children and George Nash

Logaston Press

LOGASTON PRESS
Little Logaston Woonton Almeley
Herefordshire HR3 6QH

First published by Logaston Press 1994

ISBN 1 873827 09 1

Set in Times 11/13 pt by Logaston Press
and printed in Great Britain by Ebenezer Baylis & Son, Worcester

This book is dedicated to Snoopy and Max
(Best friends to the end)

Please Note

Many of the monuments mentioned in this book are situated on private land and permission from the owner must, therefore, be obtained before visiting them. The owner's residence is given for those sites detailed in the guide sections.

All the sites covered in this book are prehistoric. Well over 70% are pre-Bronze and Iron Age and therefore there is no metal present to be located by metal detectors. To protect certain Bronze and Iron Age sites, the authors have refrained from using detailed grid references, and in the case of Neolithic stray finds, only a four figure number has been used.

The following points must be observed:

1. Always follow the Countryside Code.

2. On all sites, extreme care should be taken.

3. Any artifacts found within the county should be reported to the County Archaeological Officer, Tetbury Drive, Worcester or at any local museum.

4. Under no circumstances should visitors dig around or on any site. Any damage could result in prosecution.

5. It is an offence under the 1979 Ancient Monuments and Archaeological Areas Act to use metal detectors on or near scheduled ancient monuments. In addition, simple 'treasure hunting' near ancient monuments can well damage evidence to such an extent that archaeologists are unable to interpret it fully in the future.

Contents

Acknowledgments

Indirectly, the authors would like to thank all the historians and archaeologists who have contributed articles to the Woolhope Naturalists Field Club Transactions over the past 150 years. Be they living or dead, their efforts and enthusiasm is replicated throughout this book and without their dedication, projects such as this could not be possible.

The following people who directly helped with this book and who receive our sincere thanks are Andy Johnson, who took endless valuable time to edit and advise on certain chapters; Ann Sandford (Hereford City Museum), for access to the prehistoric collections at the museum; Ron Shoesmith, for ideas and guidance for the overall book layout; Herefordshire Aero Club, for a smooth 'ride' over the county and Duncan Brown, Sites and Monuments Records Officer for the Hereford and Worcester Archaeology Unit.

Finally, much love and thanks go to Lindsey, Sandra, Hannah, John and Jude who have shown unparalleled support and patience over the past twelve months.

George and George
July 1994

Introduction

When one looks at the Herefordshire landscape, one is struck immediately by the idyllic tranquillity of the 'black and white' villages. This is the surface. Looking further into the medieval landscape, one spies the marcher castles, and yet further back the Iron Age hillforts of greater antiquity; but very little else is visible to the casual eye of the walker, the tourist or even the historian. It may, therefore, come as a surprise to learn that, beneath the surface, Herefordshire offers the diligent explorer a rich prehistoric landscape, a landscape that contains well over a hundred scheduled ancient monuments. Hidden behind hedgerows, in deep undergrowth or found at the end of an exhausting climb, these monuments reveal a rich past and above all, allow us some insight into how our remote ancestors once lived. The monuments are their legacy. In them, past meets present, for we find that they reflect concerns that occupy our own daily lives. Thus, Neolithic chambered tombs or Bronze Age cist burials hint at religion, a suggestion that is strengthened when we discover that the people who built the tombs buried their dead with grave goods, such as decorated pottery and stone tools, to accompany them in their afterlife.

Settlements, standing stones, barrows and defensive structures are further elements in a rich mosaic of evidence which offers fascinating glimpses of many aspects of prehistoric life. To explore further the misty avenues of the prehistoric mind would require excavation. Alas, many sites within the county remain unexcavated or, sadly, were excavated and destroyed during the nineteenth and early twentieth centuries without the application of the rigorous archaeological methods in use at present.

Today, an archaeological excavation is a complex venture, employing the skills of experts from many academic and scientific fields. Those who have been involved in a dig will know that artifacts from many periods are likely to be unearthed; some sites can yield material that spans the entire range of periods, from the distant past right through to the present day. One such site is located in south Herefordshire, on the Great Doward, near Ross-on-

Wye. King Arthur's Cave possesses a history that spans at least twenty thousand years from the Upper Palaeolithic (old stone age) right through to the nineteenth century when the cave was used for iron ore extraction.

This book describes the evidence which has been found, evidence which becomes ever more slight the further back in time one goes. But we have not just used archaeological evidence, for we have coupled this with comparisons to more recent but similar societies from other parts of the world to help us add colour and tonality to a faded picture. By incorporating anthropological ideas, the book will dispel once and for all the notion that prehistory in Herefordshire is dead—it is only buried! The legacy left by our ancestors and interpreted with the aid of anthropology, is a telling reminder that these people were enterprising and passionate, that they too possessed a sense of belonging, a sense of history which they expressed in lasting form in monuments in their landscape.

The Stone Ages

Early Hunters in Herefordshire: The Upper Palaeolithic

When studying archaeological remains, the further you travel back in time the material evidence becomes more and more limited, and the problems of interpretation grow greater. This lack of evidence is compounded by the nature of the soils over much of Herefordshire—very little of an organic nature can survive for as long as ten, fifteen or even twenty thousand years in the largely acidic soil, unless it was originally deposited in a cave or rock shelter. Fortunately, Herefordshire boasts a series of caves that over the past one hundred and twenty years have revealed a detailed picture of the county's distant past.

Throughout the Upper Palaeolithic (35,000-10,000 BC) there exists an archaeological record that is dominated by flint and stone tools, but the shape, size and function of these tools say very little about the people—the most important component to the archaeologist. In order to put flesh on the story, we must both speculate and, more importantly, draw analogies from historical and contemporary sources. Obviously, this is not totally satisfactory, but at least a picture can be created of the period that is both alive and meaningful.

Throughout Britain, Early Upper Palaeolithic artifacts are, to say the least, sparse. Only a handful of sites exist, many of which are cave and rock shelters or disturbed river gravels; nearly all are located in southern Britain. However, the evidence for human activity in Herefordshire is extremely early with that for the Palaeolithic being concentrated into five small areas: Colwall, Doward (south of Ross-on-Wye), Kington, Sarnesfield (near

Weobley, and Tupsley (Hereford). However, it is only on the Doward that definite evidence of settlement in the form of caves and rock shelters has been found; the other four areas have only yielded single 'stray' flint artifacts. Thus at Tupsley, whilst a house was under construction, an impressive hand-axe was recovered from the river gravels. And here we are faced with a conundrum: either the latter finds, mainly flint blades and hand-axes, were lost during hunting expeditions or the influence of the Palaeolithic in Herefordshire was more extensive than has been imagined.

The Tupsley hand-axe

The Doward has been formed through glacial activity followed by continuous erosion by the River Wye. The caves and rock shelters are situated in a large limestone rock outcrop overlooking the Wye between Symond's Yat and the village of Ganarew. Nearly all the archaeological evidence is found either close to or within the caves and rock shelters. The two caves that have been extensively excavated, King Arthur's and Merlin's, have yielded an almost complete stratigraphic (layered) sequence that spans at least 25,000 years. Due to the good preservation qualities of the soils the sequence at Merlin's Cave includes animal bone, bone tools, a human burial, shells and, of course, flint and stone artifacts. Many of the animal bones excavated from the so-called 'Mammoth' layer at King Arthur's Cave date from the last Ice Age. The animals

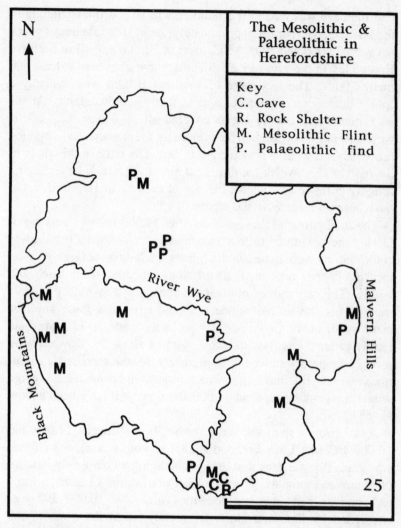

The Mesolithic &
Palaeolithic in
Herefordshire

Key
C. Cave
R. Rock Shelter
M. Mesolithic Flint
P. Palaeolithic find

River Wye

Black Mountains

Malvern Hills

25

represented in this layer suggest a landscape totally devoid of trees
and gripped by permafrost, probably similar to that of present day
southern Greenland. There are bones of the woolly rhinoceros,
horse, giant deer, wild ox, hyena and unsurprisingly because of its
name, mammoth. During the height of this Ice Age (c. 20,000 BC),
it has been suggested that the environment was far too cold for
humans. Recent radiocarbon dating carried out on human bone
from Paviland Cave (on the Gower coast in south Wales) suggests

3

that the cave was inhabited around 26,550 BC, at the beginning of the last Ice Age, but for approximately the next ten thousand years, between 27,000 and 17,000 BC, most of Britain and all of northern Europe lay in the grip of ice which in many areas was at least 400 metres thick. The landscape of southern Britain was basically a 'polar desert' and therefore, almost totally uninhabitable. At the maximum limit, the ice sheets covered all of Wales, most of the west and north Midlands, and eventually crept south and engulfed the Wash and what is now the North Sea. The edge of this sheet of ice (part of the 'Welsh Ice Cap') cut Herefordshire in half, running roughly north-south. Indeed, the site of the city of Hereford would have been under at least 300 metres of ice.

The final retreat of the ice sheets after 17,000 BC was very rapid. During the next three to four thousand years, southern Britain was colonised by sub-arctic tundra plants including sedges, grasses, mosses, lichens and small dwarf trees, notably dwarf birch and willow. This rich mosaic of plant life encouraged migratory animals such as elk, horse and reindeer. Eventually, with these animals, came small hunting communities probably made up of immediate family groups. Possibly, the cave systems along the Doward were used as temporary summer encampments, for the semi arctic conditions would still make the winter months inhospitable. Average winter temperatures around 12,000 BC may well have been as low as -5° C.

Apart from a short and very severe 'blip' between 11,000 and 10,000 BC (the Loch Lomond stadial or cold phase), the climate was gradually warming and thus encouraging a completely new set of plants and animals. The migration northwards of birch, willow and juniper and in some localities pine, by 10,000 BC was succeeded by lime and alder. Eventually, from the onset of the Mesolithic (the Middle Stone Age), oak, hazel and elm followed and flourished during the so-called 'climatic optimum' around 7,500 BC, when the average summer temperatures were at least one or two degrees higher than they are today.

Very little in the way of economic or social change is evident during the transition from the Palaeolithic to the Early Mesolithic, indeed the transition is believed to be more subtle than once thought. At King Arthur's Cave, a few of the finds suggest this

Artifacts from King Arthur's Cave, including a femur from a woolly rhinocerous, giant deer antler, badger skull, bones cracked to obtain the marrow, human finger bones, Bronze Age barbed and tanged arrowheads and Palaeolithic flint tools

subtle change as flint tools become smaller and more specialised. Examples of these microlithic blades have been found in many caves and rock shelters along the Doward, at Much Marcle, and along the ridges of Dorstone Hill and Vowchurch Common, some of which appear to have been used as arrow and spear heads which were inserted into wooden shafts.

Advanced Hunter-gatherers: The Mesolithic

The north-western European Mesolithic spans approximately five thousand years from around 10,000 BC. The onset of the Mesolithic is traditionally associated with changes in the climate and the environment. This tradition ignores changes in ideology and the gradual adaptation to new surroundings and resources. These changes could have taken well over three thousand years to complete and the dates used to express the transition between the Upper Palaeolithic and Mesolithic have to be rather arbitrary. The changes in stone technology already mentioned took place over many hundreds of years. Similarly towards the end of the Mesolithic, by approximately 4000 BC, many communities in Britain had begun to adopt small scale agriculture and what has been defined as the Neolithic period began. Changes in technology and subsequently to hunting and subsistence strategies were slow and there therefore exists a large diffuse area between the onset of the Mesolithic and its termination.

So rather than seeing change as a series of jolts, say, from hunting and gathering one day, to farming the next, transition should be regarded as a gradual affair. By the end of the Mesolithic period, society had developed into extended family groups based on permanent settlements and territories, each with their own established seasonal hunting and gathering strategy. Due to poor preservation on Mesolithic sites evidence is quite difficult to find. However, finds do show there was a strong continuity in the occupation of sites from the Late Palaeolithic through the Mesolithic and into the Early Neolithic.

Whilst there were gradual changes in technology, ideas and population, there were also changes in climate and environment. The environmental record suggests that colonisation of broad leaved woodland (also known as 'wildwood' or 'climax' woodland) was rapidly spreading from the south. One can imagine the inhabitants peering above the tree-line, and seeing smoke plumes rising from temporary settlement camp fires. Depending upon where you were, you might have been able to glimpse the tops of a few notable upland hills such as the Malverns or the Black Mountains. Within this woodland, one would smell the burning leaves and green wood from camp fires. The people from these settlements would be taking advantage of seasonal fruits, seeds and berries, whilst the

6

changing woodland had also introduced the forest dweller to new animals to hunt such as red deer, roe deer and wild pig. Causing all this change was the climate. Rising temperatures, probably eventually one or two degrees centigrade higher than today, also started to have a dramatic effect on the sea level. Over a period of about three thousand years, the sea had risen well over fifty metres and, as a result, by about 6500 BC, Britain had its land links with the continental mainland finally severed and became an island.

Nearly all Mesolithic activity is confined to south and west Herefordshire, with the majority of sites being in the late Mesolithic period (6500-3500 BC). Evidence for settlement in this period is confined to concentrations of small pieces of waste flint and flint tools called flint scatters, which can appear in two ways: stratified sites and, more commonly, surface flint scatters. Unfortunately, modern ploughing methods have, over the past fifty years, destroyed many sites that if left undisturbed could have revealed much more information. But, just to be perverse, if deep ploughing had not brought flint material to the surface, no one would have known the extent of the Mesolithic in the county.

Although stratified sites are rare, there has been flint material recovered from outside and underneath the traces of the mound which once covered Arthur's Stone on Merbach Hill above Dorstone. As we shall see, many late Mesolithic flint scatters have been discovered around the Black Mountains, not only in the Golden Valley area, but also in the upper Wye and Usk valleys. These scatters lie close to or underneath the later Neolithic chambered tombs. This could suggest a possible symbolic continuity through time: a link to an ancestral past.

Evidence for the Mesolithic in Herefordshire is concentrated in three areas: around the Golden Valley, in Ledbury (Rural) and on the Great Doward. All three areas are located close to rivers but, more importantly, to dramatic hill and mountain expanses; and are similar in distribution to the later Neolithic sites. The Black Mountains dominate the whole length of the Golden Valley, from Hay Bluff in the north to Abergavenny in the south—approximately 35 kilometres. Settlement in the valley and the surrounding hills during the late Mesolithic may be due to the symbolic importance attached to this very imposing mountain range.

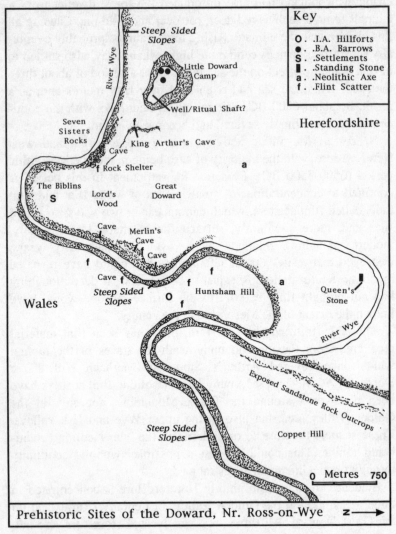

Key

O . .I.A. Hillforts
● . .B.A. Barrows
S . .Settlements
▮ . .Standing Stone
a . .Neolithic Axe
f . .Flint Scatter

Herefordshire

Steep Sided Slopes

River Wye

Little Doward Camp

Well/Ritual Shaft?

Seven Sisters Rocks

f

King Arthur's Cave

Cave

f Rock Shelter

a

The Biblins

S

Lord's Wood

Great Doward

Cave

Merlin's Cave

Cave

f

Cave f

Steep Sided Slopes

f

O

f

Huntsham Hill

a

Queen's Stone

Wales

River Wye

Exposed Sandstone Rock Outcrops

Steep Sided Slopes

Coppet Hill

0   Metres   750

Prehistoric Sites of the Doward, Nr. Ross-on-Wye   z ⟶

Mesolithic activity around the Ledbury area is more subtle. The landscape, similar to the Golden Valley, is dominated by the Malvern Hills. Surface finds are less concentrated and smaller in quantity than those from in the west of the county, suggesting either a smaller population living in isolated settlements, or highly mobile groups that took seasonal advantage of the local resources. Surface flint scatters from both these areas are confined mainly to open hill tops, heath lands and caves; very little flint has been recovered from the valley floors, indicating that the valleys were still densely wooded. Again, in both areas, Mesolithic and Neolithic flint are found in close proximity. Recent excavations (1993) near Much Marcle (10km south-west of Ledbury) have unearthed flint from both periods and reinforce the idea of continuity between Mesolithic and Neolithic communities.

Settlement evidence from the Early and Late Mesolithic on the Great Doward is confined mainly to rock shelters and caves. Within the stratigraphy (soil and sediment layers) at King Arthur's Cave and Merlin's Cave a large selection of bone and flint tools, shells, animal bones and human remains have been uncovered. A recent series of excavations in 1993 in small caves and rock shelters above the Seven Sisters rock stacks in the same area has shown that there was continuous occupation for well over fifteen thousand years, from the Upper Palaeolithic right through to the Bronze Age and beyond.

In one specific rock shelter approximately 250 metres south of King Arthur's Cave, a pierced cowrie shell was discovered. Mesolithic in date, and imported from the west coast of Britain, it probably formed part of a necklace. This object, the presence of flint in quantity, and other uncommon artifacts which have been found in the area, suggest the beginnings of a trading pattern which would gradually lead to a more advanced social system. Interestingly, very little evidence appears north of the Doward. The high concentration of flint artifacts from this area, the Golden Valley and around the Malvern Hills suggest that migration into Herefordshire came from either Gloucestershire or from central and southern Wales, probably using the main rivers and their tributaries as a means of exploration.

Why Settle in Herefordshire?

Herefordshire's late Mesolithic communities were taking full advantage of all the available woodland food resources from large foraging animals through to seasonal fruits, nuts and berries. Elsewhere, there is evidence (mainly from coastal middens—refuse dumps consisting mainly of marine shells) for the harvesting of hazelnuts, marine shells and fish. It appears the communities became spoiled for choice—the abundance of food resources, coupled with a warmer climate and improved hunting technology would have caused a rise in population.

It is most likely that settlement in Herefordshire was the result of a consolidation of prime hunting and gathering territory. This consolidation may have been due to an over-spill of population from areas to the south and west of the county. Further north and east of the county, it is possible to argue, lay dense, impenetrable woodland, whilst to the south and west, the inevitable rise in population, although leading to greater social and political complexity, might have placed an immense strain on existing resources. Herefordshire thus provided the natural next frontier territory to be colonised. It is highly probable that the rise in population not only created social complexity, but political instability with neighbouring communities, leading to the establishment of territories. In addition, by establishing a defined territory, people were creating a more permanent society. It also presupposes the advent of neighbours in what had been a wilderness.

When one talks of neighbours, one imagines a relationship that draws on communal identity, an identity that relies on social and political contact in the form of exchange or trade and common ideology as well as (in most cases) a mutual understanding of territory. Usually, these components ensure a peaceful co-existence or at least a tolerance between neighbours. The need to secure social and political alliances with neighbouring communities would be paramount to the formation of territories. It is these constraints that may have forced breakaway kinship groups in over-populated areas to migrate away from their established ancestral homelands, and beyond the territory of their neighbours.

But what of the society that was in formation? Evidence for the Upper Palaeolithic and Mesolithic periods is mostly in the form of stone and flint artifacts. But these are sparse and in order to build a better and more cohesive picture, other ideas and methods have to be used. One method is the use of ethnography, an analogy between societies and cultures of the past and those of the present, such as the bush people in southern Africa or the Eskimos from the Arctic.

As society progressed through the Mesolithic, important shifts developed within it. For example, a change in settlement behaviour occurred from the use of temporary encampments associated with moving around the countryside on hunting, gathering and foraging expeditions to more permanent bases. This change, possibly more than most others, provided the incentive to adopt agriculture, the formative process leading to the Neolithic period which was to follow. However, the abandonment of one type of economy and adoption of another cannot always be clearly identified.

One contemporary society with which an analogy can be drawn is the !Kung (San) bush people of the Kalahari desert in Namibia. Their diet consists of roughly 70% of vegetable foods, the remaining 30% is made up of mainly small invertebrate animals such as grubs and larvae, both of which are very high in protein. The hunting of large animals is only conducted on an occasional basis. Similarly, forest gatherers like the Baka people (pygmies) of central Cameroon rely heavily on gathered food, where the consumption of meat has a more symbolic role. The Baka people's 'big game', (in this case small forest monkeys) are hunted on a ritual basis, similar to that evidenced by the Australian Aborigines. In both societies everything in nature is considered sacred. Great sorrow is expressed when an animal is hunted and killed—animals are not just a source of food, but a symbolic ritual component within daily life.

Therefore, we hypothesize that animals were hunted, skinned and cooked over small camp fires throughout the wildwoods of Herefordshire. As the animal was killed, ritual chanting and dancing may have taken place, perhaps involving the reenactment of the hunt and the final kill. Sadly, one can normally only imagine these distant images. However, at the Mesolithic lowland inhabited site of Star Carr in Yorkshire, complete sets of red deer antler were recovered. Could their function have been as ceremonial masks? After all, cave art from Trois Freres in France clearly depicts a dancing human—a possible sorcerer?—wearing antlers.

Apart from a symbolic and ritual use, meat may also have possessed political significance during the Mesolithic. The equal sharing of meat in many contemporary hunter-gatherer societies dispels any notion of hierarchy or economic status; the hunting group becomes one. Again, in !Kung society the individual ownership of a killed animal cannot be regarded as possession in the true

11

sense of the word. The weapons are usually made by other individuals within the hunting party and loaned to the hunter, thus reducing his legitimate right of direct ownership of the dead animal. As a result the meat from the animal belongs to the group and the distribution allows everyone to receive a share. The traditional concept that an animal was merely caught, killed and eaten during the Mesolithic and, indeed, the Palaeolithic is probably misleading.

Throughout Europe, and most especially during the Upper Palaeolithic, animals feature most prominently in cave art. During the Mesolithic, the art form changed from being static on cave walls, to becoming portable on pieces of bone and antler. Alas, very little portable art has been found in Britain. The rumours, a few years ago, that examples of cave art had been found at Symonds Yat have proved groundless. There is locally, however, one decorated polished bone rod from King Arthur's Cave. Although some have questioned its authenticity, the decoration, most probably a simple stylized fish, is thought to be early Mesolithic (from around 8000 BC).

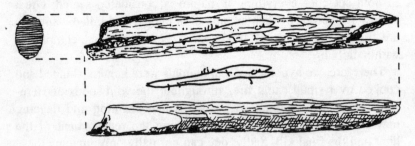

Stylised fish design on bone, from King Arthur's Cave

From this, and the few other decorated pieces from around Britain it is clear that animals feature most prominently in hunting symbolism and magic. Contemporary hunter-gatherers, and in particular the Aborigines, revere and respect individual species— kangaroo, snake, turtle and emu, to name but a few—and many of these animals feature as symbols of clan identity, sometimes depicted on bark-board paintings. The use of bark-boards and other forms of art (such as cave paintings and body adornment) creates a visual clan or family identity. The idea of clan identity and territory marking can, in many ways, be transmitted to a Mesolithic context where the concentration of large surface flint scatters in the Golden Valley area or on the Doward may represent an extended family group. Thus the distribution of flint delineates the extent of an individual Mesolithic territory, similar to the strategic distribution of chambered tombs in the Neolithic.

From Foraging to Farming: The Neolithic

The Neolithic (New Stone Age) is the latest of the three stone ages, and represents the introduction of agriculture to Britain. It is now thought that this revolution began about ten thousand years ago in the Fertile Crescent—present day Lebanon, Israel and Syria. By about 4000 BC, there is evidence that small 'garden' style allotments existed throughout the fertile valleys of western Europe, although many parts of Britain would still have been covered by dense forest. However, it seems that by this time, domesticated sheep, continental cattle, pigs and seed corn were being imported into Britain, now an island. But the introduction of agriculture was no overnight affair. During the preceding Mesolithic (10,000-3500 BC), there is evidence for the controlled herding and corralling of wild animals, in addition to the seasonal harvesting of wild fruits, roots and nuts. The rigid divide often expressed between a hunting and gathering way of life and a farming economy is in many ways misleading. Rather, the evidence suggests a gradual process of economic and social change.

Perhaps surprisingly, it is not the economic and settlement evidence that has survived the rigours of time but, for the first time, monuments commemorating the dead. Elaborate chambered tombs made of large stones, or megaliths, dominate the Neolithic landscape of Herefordshire and elsewhere. Originally, these monuments were covered by an earth mound, leaving the entrance or forecourt area and entrance passage as the only visible part. In common with present day religious buildings, areas of the tomb would have been restricted to particular social strata within the community. But archaeological evidence suggests that these chambers were more than just repositories for the dead, for the Neolithic tombs of Herefordshire—and especially those in the Golden Valley area—appear to have had a social and political as well as a symbolic function.

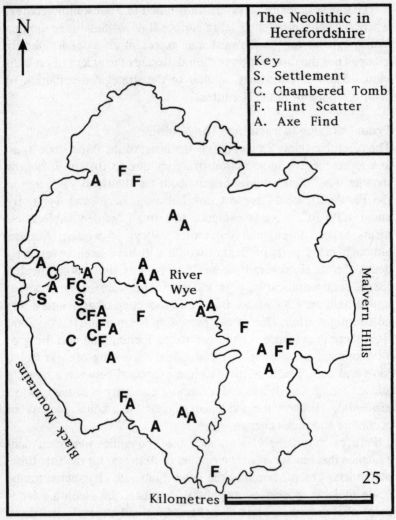

The Neolithic in Herefordshire

Key
S. Settlement
C. Chambered Tomb
F. Flint Scatter
A. Axe Find

River Wye

Malvern Hills

Black Mountains

25

Kilometres

Although few in number, Herefordshire's chambered tombs are located in two definite pockets which have yielded all the Neolithic finds in the county, including flint and polished stone axes, and flint tools. The largest of these pockets is in the Golden Valley area. Further west, but outside the county, other areas around the Black Mountains are home to more extensive Mesolithic and Neolithic activity. Indeed, at least eighteen tombs (mainly long barrows of the Severn-Cotswold tradition, a term coined to describe Late Neolithic

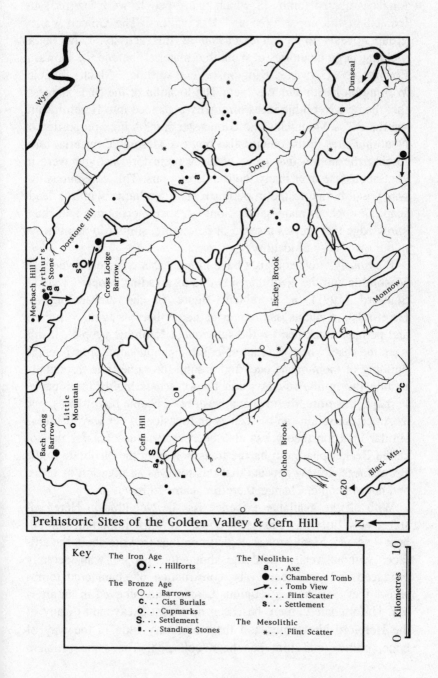

Prehistoric Sites of the Golden Valley & Cefn Hill   Z ←

Key

The Iron Age
  O . . . Hillforts

The Bronze Age
  O . . . Barrows
  c . . . Cist Burials
  o . . . Cupmarks
  S . . . Settlement
  ■ . . . Standing Stones

The Neolithic
  a . . . Axe
  ● . . . Chambered Tomb
  ↗ . . . Tomb View
  • . . . Flint Scatter
  s . . . Settlement

The Mesolithic
  * . . . Flint Scatter

0   Kilometres   10

long chambered tombs in which many people were interred) are located in the upper Wye and Usk valleys. The Golden Valley group appears to be an extension of this activity. Other areas yielding large quantities of Neolithic material include the Doward, Fownhope, Garway, Kington, Leintwardine, Much Marcle, Wellington Heath and Weobley. The location of the finds suggests that the new Neolithic ideas originally expanded into Herefordshire via the Black Mountains and Gloucestershire. A high proportion of Neolithic sites in the county also possess Mesolithic material reinforcing the notion that areas of early prehistoric activity were in continuous use over many thousands of years. This continuous use was possibly due to the importance of a familiarity with the landscape throughout many generations—a social, economic and ritual knowledge that creates a sense of belonging, similar in many ways to our own sense of identity.

Previously, archaeologists have thought that change between the Mesolithic and the Neolithic was due to invading peoples. Dr S.C. Stanford (1991), a prominent figure in the archaeology of Herefordshire claims that hunter-gatherers became 'guides, porters and perhaps stockmen for the subsequent Neolithic people'. If this were the case, where did these Neolithic people come from? As the building of monuments occurred around the same time throughout Britain the militaristic invasion theory seems highly improbable. Perhaps, therefore, the invasion was not of people but of ideas, just as Americanisation can be seen as an invasion of our way of life. A similar invasion theory has also been used to account for the so-called Beaker phase during the transition from the Neolithic to the Bronze Age. It now appears that this too was an invasion of ideas, and not of people. Change, therefore, came from within.

With all the available evidence for the Neolithic in Herefordshire, very little has been said about the most important component—people. Many archaeologists continue to write about the artifacts without really thinking about the people who actually produced and used them. The construction of chambered tombs shows that they were a religious people who believed in an afterlife. Unfortunately, there has been no recent excavation of any of the Herefordshire tombs and therefore, very little in the way of bone, pottery and flint has been collected. The same problem applies to nearly all the tombs in Wales. However, at Ty Isaf, a long chambered tomb near Talgarth, crushed bones of at least twenty individuals together with Neolithic pottery, a polished stone axe and a selection of flint arrowheads (all, presumably, grave goods) were discovered. Similar methods of burying the dead are practiced all over the world today, and even in Victorian Britain the dead were often interred with small items of jewelry. Finally they were prepared and dressed for the journey to the after-life.

Attempting an understanding of the living is more difficult. Very little organic material such as arrow shafts, buckets and canoes, animal products like skins, tooth pendants and bone mattock handles and, finally, food remains have survived.

Apart from the more obvious structures, such as Arthur's Stone, Cross Lodge Barrow and, possibly, Dunseal, Bach and Park Wood long barrows, the Golden Valley area also has a number of standing stones which are possibly of Late Neolithic or Early Bronze Age date. In addition, large quantities of flints have been recovered mainly as a result of deep furrow ploughing which has brought Neolithic flint, Mesolithic and Bronze Age material to the surface. As with many other areas of high Neolithic activity, Herefordshire has very little evidence of settlement. However, on Dorstone Hill, equidistant between Arthur's Stone and Cross Lodge Barrow there is an extensive Neolithic settlement, one of only three which have been recognized in Herefordshire. This settlement lies on the edge of an escarpment and commands views across the Wye Valley to the north and the Golden Valley to the south. Excavated between 1965 and 1970, this eighteen acre site produced well over 4,000 pieces of flint. Also found were polished stone axes, pottery, storage pits, hut floors and evidence of a low wall and fence stockade. The flint material recovered suggests at least contact and possibly trade with the Cotswolds and south Wales. Large quantities of flint material have also been discovered along the western ridges of Merbach Hill, Dorstone Hill and Vowchurch Common. Further west, on the top of Cefn Hill, another possible settlement has been uncovered, again as a result of ploughing. Here, leaf-shaped arrowheads, spindle-whorls, a sandstone mortar and a pebble hammerstone were discovered in a shallow depression, beneath a thin layer of peat.

Prestige and the Axe

Scattered around the north, south and west of the county are single 'prestige' finds that could indicate either possible trading alliances or seasonal expeditions outside Herefordshire. These prestige goods, approximately forty in total, consist of polished stone and flint axes. Why prestige? It has been shown that if used, most polished stone axes would almost instantly shatter. However, by shaping and polishing an axe from stone an item is created which, although in theory functional, in fact symbolises power and prestige and, above all, a stratified society. An assumption can be made, therefore, that both flint and polished stone axes are status symbols owned and controlled by the most powerful. The origins of such prestige items suggests trade with areas as far away as Cumbria and Cornwall, and maybe even southern Scandinavia. Two fine examples of Greenstone axes have been found in the county at Elton and St Margarets, the Greenstone originating from the Penzance area. Axes from Great Langdale in Cumbria and from Gwynedd have been found at Almeley and Weobley respectively. It is not known if these axes were shaped in the source areas or within Herefordshire itself, although there is evidence of extensive flint waste material being deposited around Great Langdale in Cumbria, suggesting that rough casts were made at source and later re-worked in the home locality. The archaeologist Stephen Briggs suggested in 1973 that, at least during the early Neolithic, the material used for creating stone axes may have originated from glacial erratics that had been transported and deposited by ice during the last glacial advance some 18,000 years ago from areas such as Cumbria, north Wales and the Pennines. Although this may be possible, it does not allow for imported flint from Wiltshire and stone from Cornwall, both areas lying to the south of the ice margin. The only way of importing such flint into the county would have been through contact and exchange with other groups, or by mounting expeditions. In addition, it can be argued that in order to add prestige to an axe, the flint or stone used in its manufacture must have come direct from the source area.

By employing time in axe expeditions, society was creating a restricted and exclusive supply and demand—cheap imitations were not good enough, even if some were made from shale and

Polished stone and flint Neolithic axes from west Herefordshire

mudstone. This would have made pointless the use of glacial erratics to make prestige items, especially when glacial deposits are so abundant on the valley floors and slopes of Herefordshire. Developing this theme further, it is likely that the organisation of trade expeditions of a long duration during the middle and late Neolithic would have been socially and politically complex. They could not have been undertaken by small scale agricultural groups. Indeed, judging by the extent of Neolithic monuments and surface flint and stone found in Herefordshire (and neighbouring areas to the south and west), the organisation would have been large scale, possibly involving an alliance between a number of groups bound together by kinship and/or a common ancestry.

It is then logical to suppose that the people co-operated enough to form recognizable territories—but what is the evidence on the ground? The extent of the Neolithic in Herefordshire is well defined with Neolithic clusters located mainly in the west of the county. These clusters could represent possible territories each with its own nucleated settlement of which the Dorstone Hill settlement is a fine example. In all, eleven clusters exist within Herefordshire's two main Neolithic areas.

All these clusters appear to have three major similarities. Firstly, each is located near a major river or stream. Secondly, all are positioned close to large hills and mountains. Finally, many have both earlier and later settlement evidence suggesting a long continuity of occupation. This continuity of settlement could be due to a number of components. The most obvious of these is economic, due to an abundance of available resources. Similarly, there is the socio-political component, providing support and mutual defence under extreme threat. Possibly, the most important component is symbolic. This was probably created from a common religious ancestral ideology incorporating both landscape and economic resources—similar to the integral symbolism bound-in with the sacred land rites of the Australian Aborigines. What is most probable, is that such continuous settlement may well incorporate all of these components.

Symbolism and the Black Mountains
The eastern edge of the Black Mountains now forms part of the natural boundary between Wales and Herefordshire. Of the up to 18 chambered tombs scattered around these mountains, two definite and four possible ones are found in Herefordshire. The questionable sites include a barrow at Dunseal, and long barrows at Bach, Garway and at Park Wood. All these sites are located along the eastern edge of the Golden Valley area. In addition to the Herefordshire tombs there are a number of standing stones which have debatable origins and dates, and at least six extensive occupation areas, as well as numerous stray finds. Both the occupation sites and the monuments appear to be deliberately positioned in order to keep the mountains in full view. A similar pattern occurs in the upper Usk and Wye valleys—the Black Mountains seem to act as a visual magnet to which Neolithic communities were drawn. Symbolically, the mountains could have acted as a religious nucleus. Any settlement further east and outside the draw of the mountains may well have been considered symbolically dangerous and strictly taboo. However, the mountains themselves may have

*Neolithic leaf-shaped arrowheads from
the Golden Valley and Cefn Hill*

been seen as dangerous and mysterious, for very little Neolithic material has been found on them. By siting a settlement close to the mountains it would be possible to create a sense of belonging with the landscape—communities could change a space into a place and establish an identity, an identity that in turn would create a territory.

It is noticeable that many monuments within the western part of the county are located around the edges of high Neolithic activity and it is possible, therefore, that these monuments represent territorial markers as well as providing a place for the dead. For example, by locating monuments around the extremes of the Golden Valley area a defined territory could be established. As very little in the way of surface flint material has been found in the immediate areas outside the valley, it is arguable that the surrounding hills, the valley slopes and the rich fertile valley floor provided for all the needs of an organised Neolithic community. Similar patterns occur further west, on Cefn Hill. Here both settlement and monuments appear to be spatially organised within the landscape, and all are deliberately orientated towards the Black Mountains.

The other core Neolithic area in Herefordshire, close to the market town of Ledbury, has a number of extensive lithic scatters but no evidence of structures, although there are two possible long barrows, one at Fownhope and one in Holme Lacy Park. In common with the Golden Valley area, the flint scatters show continuous activity from the Mesolithic to the Bronze Age and beyond. This area too, has a dramatic hill range nearby—the Malvern Hills—and all the major flint scatters are on sites which have the Malverns in full view. Similar to the Black Mountains, no structures or flint material have been found on the Malvern Hills themselves. However, the siting of structures on upland areas was to change during the Early Bronze Age.

Arthur's Stone

Neolithic long barrow
Some of the upright stones and part of the capstone are still in situ
Location: 2km to the east of Dorstone & signposted (SO 319 431)
Access: By the side of a minor road

Arthur's Stone is signposted from the A438, Hereford to Brecon road, near Staunton-on-Wye, and from the B4248 Madley to Hay-on-Wye road at the edge of Dorstone. From Dorstone Arthur's Stone lies approximately 2km up a steep and narrow lane, and just over the summit of the hill you turn left.

This Neolithic long barrow, probably the most famous of all the prehistoric monuments in Herefordshire, is on Merbach Hill, some 280m above sea level. Arthur's Stone dates from about 3500 BC and is one of the most northerly chambered tombs of the Severn-Cotswold Group (a series of about 200 Middle and Late Neolithic corporate monuments scattered all over the south-west Midlands and central Wales). It is one of possibly five tombs that dominate the Neolithic landscape of the northern reaches of the Golden Valley. Originally set in an oval mound (some 26m x 17m), this tomb has nine upright stones (forming a polygonal chamber), an unorthodox right-angled passage and a enormous capstone, estimated to weigh over 25 tonnes. The sheer size and weight of the uprights and capstone suggest that the construction time was long and involved the labour of a large number of people. Bill Startin (1981) has argued that a tomb such as Arthur's Stone might take at least 7,000 and possibly 16,000 labour hours.

The tomb has long entered local folklore. One story suggests it is so-named because King Arthur is believed to have fought a desperate battle here with another king; Arthur was killed and laid to rest inside the chamber. Another story tells of a battle between Arthur and a giant. The giant was slain and fell onto the stones with his knees or elbows (depending on which version) creating hollows in the stones. This story also explains why the capstone is split into two pieces! The Quoit Stone is located 2m southwest of the chamber and also has 'hollows'. It was once believed that this stone was used in the game of quoits and that the hollows were made by the players' heels. We now know, however, that they are 'cupmarks'.

Very little is known about the origin of these cupmarks—some suggest that they are a Bronze Age phenomenon, possibly incorporated as an act of defacement or connected with the reuse of the monument for social/political rather than burial/ritual purposes. On one of the uprights 12 cupmarks have been identified. Cupmarks are a rare phenomenon in Herefordshire where only three other monuments definitely have them: Kinsham Standing Stone, 17km north of Arthur's Stone which has seven; the standing stone close to Dorstone village and the Queen's Stone on the Doward. All three are believed to date from the Early Bronze Age. Cupmarks are also found on a small standing stone at St Weonards, but this monument has been removed, possibly stolen, in the recent past.

The capstone, which is split into two pieces, is orientated NE-SW with the south-western end pointing towards the southern section of the Golden Valley. The chamber has, at its western end, a false portal stone (partly blocking the doorway to the main chamber) and a passage that is orientated north. However, the passage changes direction to the north-west, pointing towards the impressive Hay Bluff, the northern extent of the Black Mountains. The unorthodox redirection of the passage and the orientation of the capstone might

24

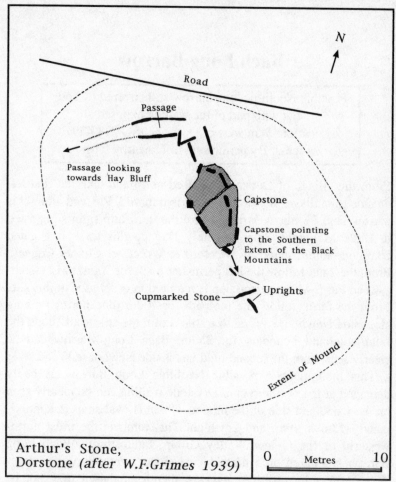

N

Road

Passage

Passage looking
towards Hay Bluff

Capstone

Capstone pointing
to the Southern
Extent of the Black
Mountains

Cupmarked Stone — Uprights

Extent of Mound

Arthur's Stone,
Dorstone *(after W.F.Grimes 1939)*

0   Metres   10

suggest that Arthur's Stone was positioned deliberately to encompass the whole aspect of the Black Mountains. But why? One can
only make tenuous assumptions. One idea is that the Black
Mountains were incorporated into the social and symbolic identity
of these first farming settlers to help create a sense of belonging.
Indeed, many other tombs in the upper Wye and Usk valleys appear
to be positioned to encompass views of the mountains.

Mesolithic flint has been found underneath and around Arthur's
Stone and Gwernvale, near Crickhowell. The latter also has flint
and chert material from the Late Upper Palaeolithic (c.10,000 BC).
So, even during the Neolithic, Arthur's Stone would have possessed
a 'history' and, more importantly, an affinity with the local population's ancestors.

Bach Long Barrow

Possible Neolithic long barrow still covered by soil,
but with part of the walling exposed
Location: 5km west of Dorstone (SO 277 429)
Access: By permission from nearby farm

From the village of Dorstone, proceed north and take the first left outside the village, signposted to Mynyddbrydd. Proceed along this narrow lane for about 3km and take the third turn right signposted to Little Mountain. Approximately 1km up this track is a gated common, administered by Hereford & Worcester County Council. From the gate, follow the left perimeter track for 500m to Llanerch-y-Coed Farm where permission is required in order to visit this site. From the farm, follow the footpath for 400m (due north) running alongside Newhouse Wood to a stile. From the stile walk along the field/woodland boundary for 250m. Bach Long Barrow can be clearly seen from the second field just inside Newhouse Wood.

This monument, a possible Neolithic Long Barrow, is badly damaged at the northern end. Drystone walling can be clearly seen on the woodland side of the mound, which is oval-shaped, approximately 13m x 10m, and 2m high. This tomb is the most north-westerly of the Golden Valley Group. Interestingly, Bach Long Barrow is located on a north facing slope, overlooking the upper Wye Valley. Its position suggests, therefore, that it may not be associated with any of the Golden Valley tombs. The location and localised orientation (E-W) suggests an association with nearby Clyro Court Farm Long Barrow and the now damaged Clyro Long Barrow, both just over the border in Powys. All three tombs have dominant views over the upper Wye Valley and all are intervisible. Unfortunately, dense woodland to the north of Bach Long Barrow makes it difficult to ascertain if there is intervisibility with other monuments.

Cross Lodge Barrow

Major Neolithic long barrow
Location: 300m from a B road, 1km south of Dorstone
(SO 333 417)
Access: By permission from nearby farm

Located about 2km south-east of Arthur's Stone, Cross Lodge Barrow lies on a small ridge, half way up Dorstone Hill on private land. From the village of Dorstone, proceed south-east for 1km along the B 4348 towards the village of Peterchurch. Obscured by a boundary hedge, Cross Lodge Long Barrow, with its three ash trees, is located in the corner of a field, approximately 300m from the road, opposite Llanafon Farm, from where permission to walk to the site is required.

Possibly much larger during the Neolithic period, the mound is now an elongated oval shape, approximately 18m x 10m and 2.5m high. Locally orientated (NW-SE) towards the Golden Valley, Cross Lodge Long Barrow (as with Arthur's Stone) embraces a commanding view of the Black Mountains. During the recent past, the monument has suffered plough damage to the northern section of the mound. Indeed, a large number of stones now litter the corner of the field, some of which may belong to the original tomb structure.

During the Neolithic, Cross Lodge Long Barrow would have been visible from the valley floor as well as from any settlement within the northern part of the Golden Valley, unlike Arthur's

Stone. Discovered between the two tombs in the early 1960s was a large Neolithic settlement, located on a prominent spur. The settlement is visible from and central to both tombs; however, there is no intervisibility between the tombs. Both the positioning of the settlement and the tombs appear to be deliberate.

Arthur's Stone and Cross Lodge Long Barrow are constructed in different ways, which suggests either that the monuments were built at different times or may represent two different meanings. Cross Lodge Barrow is aligned to the orientation of the valley whereas Arthur's Stone may represent a valley-end territorial marker. This being the case, were both tombs in use at the same time? It is likely that Arthur's Stone is considerably earlier than Cross Lodge Long Barrow and, judging by the size and construction of Cross Lodge Long Barrow, the time and labour input for the latter would have been much less. Obviously, construction time would depend upon the availability of local materials such as sandstone and the labour needed to transport the blocks across the countryside. This being the case, the spare time available to the first farmers must have been considerable. Tomb building may have possibly been undertaken during the winter months when there was no growing season. Alternatively, it may have been the initial task undertaken by the first settlers in the valley in order to establish their territory and to develop a sense of belonging to the area.

Dorstone Hill Neolithic Settlement

Site of a Neolithic settlement
Location: 2km east of Dorstone (SO 326 423)
Access: By permission from nearby farm

From Dorstone Church, take the road south towards Peterchurch and near the edge of the village take the narrow lane off to the left signposted Arthur's Stone. Before the brow of the hill, and just before a small coppice on the right, is a large field. The settlement is located in the south-eastern corner of this field, just behind the Dorstone Hill promontory hillfort. Before visiting this site, permission is required from Upper Bodcot Farm located on the right-hand side after taking the left-hand turn signposted to Arthur's Stone.

This settlement, probably one of at least three in the Golden Valley and Cefn Hill areas, covers approximately 7.2 hectares, and is equidistant from Arthur's Stone and Cross Lodge Long Barrow. The site was discovered by field walkers during the 1950s and 60s, and was later excavated by C. Houlder and W.R. Pye between 1965 and 1970.

The settlement was enclosed on the west side by a crude stone wall, on top of which was a wooden stockade fence. Also present were storage pits (possibly used for grain), occupation floors and undisturbed 'buried (occupation) soils', ideal for dating. Fragments of pottery and waste flint were found within this soil. The vast amounts of flint recovered, over 4,000 pieces, indicates that the site was Neolithic. In addition pottery and over 50 polished stone axe fragments were uncovered. The stone and flint was imported from as far away as south Wales and the Cotswolds.

The size of this settlement suggests that a large population occupied the upland areas of the Golden Valley. In constructing this village, plus the two nearby tombs, the authors have calculated, by considering the hours required to build the tombs and maintain the settlement, and by comparison to evidence gained from the Iron Age hillforts, that the population must have been in excess of 250 people. The slopes, ridges and tops of the eastern uplands, from Merbach Hill in the north-east to Canns Hill in the south were being used for settlement and the construction of burial monuments. Fertile woodland on the valley floor would be slowly cleared through the Neolithic period for allotment-style agriculture. More land would be utilised as the population grew. Red deer and wild boar would be hunted in the pockets of dense woodland scattered throughout the valley, just as their ancestors had done a thousand years before during the Mesolithic. By settling on the eastern hills, the inhabitants had full views over the Golden Valley and, more importantly, over the Black Mountains with their possible symbolic importance.

During the Late Neolithic and Early Bronze Age there is evidence throughout southern Britain that political instability and, in some cases, open warfare occurred. This would help account for the strategic position and stone and wooden wall around the village, and the equivalent settlement on Cefn Hill, 10km due west.

Dunseal Long Barrow

Intact Neolithic long barrow
Location: 9km south-east of Dorstone,
2.5km north of Abbey Dore(SO 391 338)
Access: By permission from nearby farm

Take the Kerry's Gate turn off the B4347, Kingstone to Abbey Dore road, approximately 3km from the junction with the B4348. Proceed along this narrow country lane for about 1.5km. On the left, immediately opposite Cwm Farm, is a small grassed track leading to Dunseal Farm. Permission is required from this farm to visit the site. From the farm, walk 200m up a steep hill. Dunseal Long Barrow, still very much intact (and unexcavated) can be clearly seen along a narrow ridge, in a corner of a small field. To the right of the tomb is Dunseal Wood. From here, there are outstanding views of the lower part of the Golden Valley and the Black Mountains.

This monument and the now destroyed Park Wood chambered tomb mark the most southerly extent of Neolithic influence in the Golden Valley. Possibly, Dunseal Long Barrow and Park Wood represent territorial boundary markers. Beyond these monuments, southwards, there are no other monuments and very few artifacts.

The dating of the site is still a little uncertain. The few surface finds (from ploughing) suggest a Neolithic or Early Bronze Age date. The mound itself is oval, approximately 27m x 14m at its longest and widest points and 2m high. It has been suggested that the mound may have once been circular, hinting towards a Bronze Age date. However, the authors tend to think that, owing to its location (high on a west facing ridge with commanding views, especially to the south and west) this monument can be none other than a Neolithic Long Barrow. Its location, similar to other burial monuments in the Golden Valley area, reinforces this idea.

The size of the mound suggests that the monument is indeed large, in fact similar in size to Arthur's Stone, possibly even of equal importance. We would hazard a guess and suggest that Dunseal too, has an enormous capstone supported by a number of uprights. Who knows of the many secrets which may be revealed by excavation, all of which have remained entombed for well over 5,000 years. Elsewhere, excavations have uncovered many new ideas about the first farmers. At Ty Isaf, near Talgarth in Powys, archaeologists discovered the crushed bones of at least seventeen individuals, along with pottery, leaf-shaped arrowheads and a polished axe. More recently in 1972, from the long chambered tomb at Penywrlod, also near Talgarth, and once quarried for its stone, numerous flint artifacts were recovered, along with a bone flute, pottery and the bones of at least eleven individuals, as well as those of cattle, sheep, pig, red deer and wild horse.

King Arthur's Cave

Cave showing occupation from the Upper Palaeolithic through to
the Bronze Age and beyond
Location: 8km from Monmouth, 13km from Ross (SO 546 156)
Access: Via a public footpath from a public car park.
Forestry Commission rules and regulations apply
when visiting this site.

This cave can be approached from either Monmouth or Ross-on-
Wye via the A40. Take the turning, 4km from Monmouth, signposted Doward). Follow the road across the A40 to Ganarew and
turn left at the T junction—the road now running parallel to the
A40. After 600m take the first right, again signposted Doward (and

Heritage Centre). Proceed along this extremely narrow and winding road for about 2km and turn right onto a rough forest track. Approximately 200m from this turning is a small car park. From the car park, walk back towards the track turning. There is a small footpath on the left. Carefully walk down this path, past a disused quarry and a series of rock overhangs. The footpath continues past three large rock shelters (at least one of these rock shelters may be mistaken for King Arthur's Cave). Follow the footpath for 250m and King Arthur's Cave is located at the end of this rock outcrop. In front of the cave is a large earthen ridge—the spoil heap from the 1927 excavation. The cave itself is recognised by a large double entrance.

King Arthur's Cave was extensively excavated in 1870/1, 1925/ 27 and 1954/55. Prior to this, the cave was used for iron ore extraction during the eighteenth and nineteenth centuries which destroyed most of the archaeological evidence. However, the 1870/71 excavations revealed that the sediment stratigraphy around the cave walls and the central column that divides the two cave sections (close to the entrance) was virtually undisturbed. The material recovered from this section revealed finds that span the period from the Early Upper Palaeolithic (latter part of the Old Stone Age) to the Bronze Age (c.2000 BC), a total of some 50,000 years.

The five distinct stratified layers represent a series of cold (glacial) and warm (interglacial) episodes. The upper cave surface (most recent) consists of a stalactite floor. Associated with this layer were the remains of badger, birds and fox. Also present were a small number of pottery sherds, probably of Bronze Age date.

The second layer consists of an upper cave earth, 0.6m thick. Intermixed with this layer were the bones of horse, cave bear and beaver as well as flint material dating back to the Upper Palaeolithic. Below this, a third layer, approximately one metre deep revealed evidence of possible glacial activity (suggesting that the ice margin was close by). The presence of red sand and, more importantly, rolled pebbles suggest that debris from the nearby old red sandstone outcrops on Coppet Hill and Huntsham Hill had been transported west, down the Wye Valley, past King Arthur's Cave. Alternatively, this layer may have been formed by the water seepage which carried debris through fissures from the surrounding

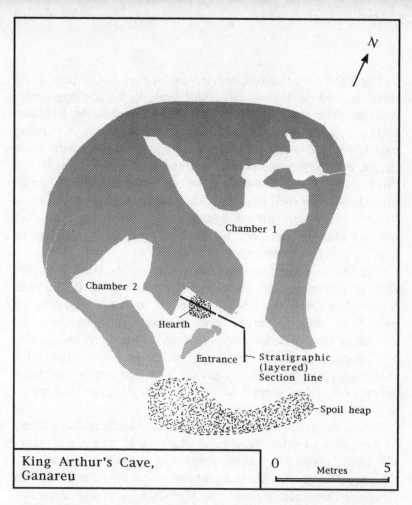

Chamber 1

Chamber 2

Hearth

Entrance — Stratigraphic
(layered)
Section line

Spoil heap

King Arthur's Cave,
Ganareu

0   Metres   5

porous rocks. The fourth layer, a late glacial deposit, consisted of hearth material (charcoal and ash) incorporating remains of giant elk, horse and ox, as well as further Upper Palaeolithic flints including scrapers and blades. The fifth layer, approximately 6 metres down and aptly named the 'mammoth' layer, was formed by a lower and ancient cave-earth. In amongst this layer were the remains of mammoth, elk, reindeer and woolly rhinoceros. Some of the bones had possibly been gnawed by hyenas, meaning that at one point in the cave's early history it might have been inhabited by hyenas, cave bears and other mammals. This being the case, Upper Palaeolithic hunter-gatherers would have certainly used this cave on a temporary basis rather than on a permanent one! Also present were large quantities of flint dated to the Upper Palaeolithic.

The 1926/7 excavations directed by Herbert Taylor provided a more detailed report on the available stratigraphy. Six layers were discovered: three Upper Palaeolithic, one Mesolithic, one Neolithic and a recently formed 'stalactite' floor. Although correlating closely with the sequences uncovered by Symonds some fifty years before, they were better defined and above all, intact. In total, 720 pieces of flint were recovered as well as numerous pieces of bone. Indeed, even the spoil heap from the 1870/1 excavation was excavated! Here, many artifacts were recovered including a possible tranchet axe, flint scrapers, burins (awls) and large quantities of flint flake and waste material.

The origin of the flint is difficult to establish. No fine quality flint is known locally, therefore it would appear that it was imported, probably from South Wales. If so, either long distance trade with other groups or long distance expeditions to areas containing flint would have been necessary. Judging by the quantity of flint recovered, that incidentally spans the Upper Palaeolithic right through to the Bronze Age, the exchange and/or expedition networks would have been well established, using the local waterways and ancient tracks.

Also recovered were a number of bone and antler artifacts. Many of these were used for digging and chopping. However, one particular piece, a bone rod, was decorated with a possible 'stylised' fish design. Although now considered to be of questionable origin, this design is nevertheless similar to Mesolithic 'portable' decorated artifacts from southern Scandinavia.

Herbert Taylor's excavation uncovered two hearths, both crammed full with valuable bone deposits. The first hearth had been used and reused over many thousands of years and contained bones of ox, deer, pig, horse, beaver, brown bear and hedgehog. Also present were many tools including 'imported' pebbles. These were used as either hammerstones or polishing/rubbing stones for the production of tools. Other pebbles were present in many colours, though particularly red and green. Their function is unknown, but it has been suggested that they were decorative.

Below the first hearth was a thin yellow soil layer. This too, revealed both flint and bone evidence. Obviously older than the first hearth, this layer revealed yet more evidence of animals, including now extinct giant deer, together with ox, wild horse, hare, pika, lemming and hedgehog.

The second hearth, 0.3m thick, was again very rich in bone material. Present were giant deer, horse, ox and pika. Some of the bone had been split longitudinally in order for the then cave dwellers to extract valuable protein enriched marrow. Along with the bone material were large amounts of burnt flint including scrapers, points and blades. All the flint material from both hearths is very similar in form to other Upper Palaeolithic cave sites on the Gower Coast and in the Mendip Hills.

So, one can imagine these hearths being a focal point for our ancestral hunter-gatherers and where the day's catch, probably a deer or wild horse, was cooked at night. Stories which had been passed down from generation to generation were told as they devoured the succulent meal. Possibly, meat and flint were 'offered' to the fire as a way of thanking the deities for providing a good kill.

Whilst there were no results published of the 1954/5 excavation, a recent survey in the Doward area in 1993 has confirmed that the prehistory of this cave and other neighbouring caves and rock shelters is indeed complex. The continuous human presence, especially during the late Upper Palaeolithic and early Mesolithic (10,000-8,000 BC), is a vital key to the colonisation and subsequent settlement of south and west Herefordshire.

Merlin's Cave

Cave showing occupation from the Upper Palaeolithic
through to the Bronze Age and beyond
Location: 13km from Ross, 8km from Monmouth (SO 556 153)
Access: Via a public footpath from a public car park.
Forestry Commission rules and regulations apply
when visiting this site

From the car park above King Arthur's Cave (for directions to this
car park please refer to the entry for King Arthur's Cave), proceed
for 1.5km along a forestry track towards The Biblins (a youth

adventure centre). From The Biblins, turn left onto a track that follows the course of the River Wye. The track soon becomes a narrow footpath which you follow for 400m. Directly left is a steep incline. The entrance to Merlin's Cave is in two sections: a lower chamber and an alcove. Together, they can be clearly seen approximately 60m up the slope (the entrance resembles the 'eye sockets' of a human skull). Extreme caution should be observed when climbing up to this cave.

South facing, Merlin's Cave is located on an enormous rock outcrop, one of many with numerous caves and rock shelters that encompass the whole of the Doward meander; from the jutting rock stacks of the Seven Sisters to Symonds Yat. The caves were formed by water seeping and eroding through carboniferous limestone rock fissures.

Merlin's Cave, like King Arthur's Cave, was thoroughly excavated in the late 1920s by T.F. Hewer of the University of Bristol Spelaeological Society, who also gave it its name. Sadly, both Merlin's and Arthur's Caves were exploited for iron ore during the eighteenth and nineteenth centuries which has damaged the archaeological evidence for earlier times. Indeed, there is evidence of much earlier iron ore extraction at both caves during the Roman period. Despite this, however, both caves have evidence of a human presence throughout prehistory; certainly as far back as the Late Upper Palaeolithic (15-10,000 BC), though at Merlin's Cave, very little Upper Palaeolithic material has been recovered. Only a handful of flint artifacts have been found of which a schoolboy's find, a Bronze Age razor, is the most notable. At the back of the cave, Hewer's team uncovered the remains of a possible burial, although it was difficult to date. Numerous bone artifacts were also recovered including a bone point (sheep), a perforated tooth (dog or fox) and two bone spatulas. Also found were two perforated amber beads and small chippings of chert which were either Mesolithic or Upper Palaeolithic in date. Pottery was also present—a small collection of Bronze Age Beaker and Roman black burnished pottery sherds. Finally, a fourth century Roman coin was found, dating from the period of Constantine the Great, AD 330-335.

Within the cave earths was a large collection of bone material which had been built up over many thousands of years. This bone

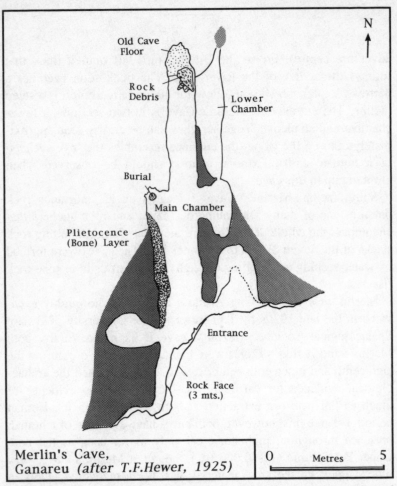

Old Cave
Floor

Rock
Debris

Lower
Chamber

Burial

Main Chamber

Plietocence
(Bone) Layer

Entrance

Rock Face
(3 mts.)

Merlin's Cave,
Ganareu *(after T.F.Hewer, 1925)*

0   Metres   5

material gives a unique insight to past climatic and environmental change. These bones along with water action, cave earths, limestone and rock debris have created a conglomerate platform located against the left wall, near the cave entrance. It is approximately 4.5m long and at least 1.4m thick. Previous investigations have revealed that cave inhabitants included common lemming, Arctic lemming, European beaver, bank vole, short-tailed vole, northern vole, field vole and numerous birds. The presence of some of these small mammals suggest that the climate was a good deal colder than today, possibly that of a tundra-scrub environment, void of any trees.

The Bronze Age

It would appear that the Bronze Age began very much as it ended—during a period of turmoil in which the old social order was undermined and eventually yielded to a new kind of society. At the Bronze to Iron Age transition, the new social order was the 'heroic' society of Celtic Europe. But, seventeen hundred years earlier, as metal first began to replace stone as the material for tools and weapons, we encounter Europe's first 'chiefs'—powerful, entrepreneurial individuals who were singled out for special treatment at death. The new aristocrats were often interred with their personal regalia—beads, welt (hem) fittings, pendants and pins—a visual expression of power and status. Their memorials were earthen mounds or 'barrows', among the most conspicuous Bronze Age relics in Herefordshire. Barrows replaced the large, austere, group monuments, such as Arthur's Stone, which were blocked up and abandoned to the elements.

Two barrow burials, each containing an individual in a stone cist, were brought to the surface by ploughing in the Olchon Valley. One of the cists, which was made from slabs of local sandstone, contained the well preserved skeleton of a man aged between 25 and 30. The man was interred in a crouching position, his head facing north. At his feet was placed a barbed and tanged arrowhead, and in the grave was—significantly—a single clay 'beaker'.

At one time it was believed that the small, highly decorated beakers found under round barrows came to Britain sometime towards the end of the third millennium BC as part of an 'invasion package' which also included copper daggers, stone wrist-guards, v-perforated buttons, double pointed awls and barbed and tanged arrowheads. The Continental tribal groups who introduced this package were labelled Beaker Folk, and it was argued that they first entered eastern Britain from Holland.

Today the tendency is to view the invasion as one of ideas rather than of actual peoples—ideas which the fashion-conscious eagerly took up. The earliest beakers were the finest, and it is conceivable that they were imported. Thereafter, the standard declined, with local copies becoming much more prevalent. The Olchon Valley example is one such local imitation and its presence indicates that those who buried what is presumed to be the body of a young noble were in touch with the latest mortuary practice to spread from Europe.

The beakers themselves were probably used as drinking vessels as well as burial goods, and ritual drinking during the interment could well have been part of the beaker cult. This cult may have brought Herefordshire within a single cultural and political region extending from the Wash in the east to Cardigan Bay in the west. Certainly, there is evidence from that time that local elites exchanged gifts with communities in the far west of Britain.

Another cist burial of the Olchon Valley type was discovered north of Brinsop Court, near Mansell Lacy. Although the burial was badly damaged, consisting of only a few pieces of stone walling and bone, it was apparent that the body had been laid out with the same north-south orientation found in the Olchon Valley.

A further example was discovered in 1992 at Aymestry Quarry, to the south of Pyon Wood hillfort. Here a stone cist was again found to contain a human skeleton and beaker. All were probably originally covered by barrows. Though only these few have been investigated, 26 such barrows are known in Herefordshire. Wider evidence from across Britain shows that the goods buried in beaker graves differentiate between male and female occupants, that is, graves are 'gender encoded'. Males are consistently buried with barbed and tanged arrowheads, linking them to warfare, while females are exclusively associated with jewellry and domestic items.

Unlike the majority of the earlier Neolithic tombs, barrows are sited either on the tops of hills or on the valley floor, close to the flood plain. Many hilltop barrows cannot be seen from the surrounding valleys, suggesting they were purposely hidden.

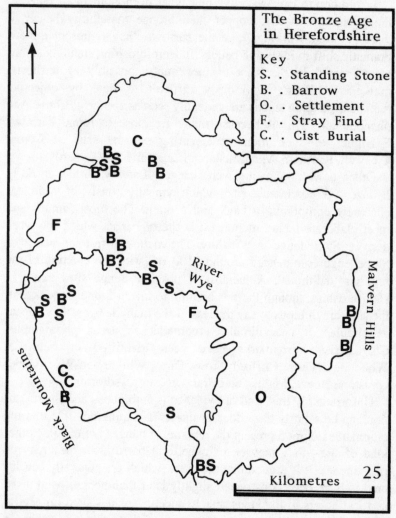

N

The Bronze Age
in Herefordshire

Key
S. . Standing Stone
B. . Barrow
O. . Settlement
F. . Stray Find
C. . Cist Burial

C

B
S
B S
B

B
B

F

B B
B?
S
B S

River
Wye

S B S
B S
B S

F

C C
B

S

O

B
B
B

Malvern Hills

Black Mountains

B S

Kilometres   25

Examples include the Shire Ditch barrows on the summit of the
Malverns at Colwall, Titley Barrow, Longtown Barrow or cairn and
the barrows on Cefn Hill.

Interestingly, the Central Herefordshire Basin is virtually devoid
of Early Bronze Age monuments presumably due to its coverage by
dense forest. It was not until the Late Bronze Age or Early Iron Age
that this central area of the county began to be utilized by prehistoric people.

In addition to barrows, other new types of monument appeared in the landscape as first copper then bronze metallurgy began to displace stone-working. Like the barrows, they represent quite a dramatic shift in ideas and beliefs. In Herefordshire, standing stones were erected in the west of the county, possibly as territorial markers. Although notoriously difficult to date by objective methods, standing stones are generally seen as an Early Bronze Age phenomenon. This is because many are close to round barrows. Examples of such monument pairing can be seen at Comb, Craswall, Kinsham, Michaelchurch Escley and St Weonards.

Other new monuments were henges, Late Neolithic or Early Bronze Age ceremonial sites which typically consist of a circular enclosure comprising a bank and a ditch. The most famous and most elaborate henge monument is the one from which the word derives: Stonehenge in Wiltshire. The main construction period at Stonehenge commenced around 2100 BC with the erection of the familiar 'trilithons'. A handful of possible henge sites exists in Herefordshire, though there is nothing to match Stonehenge and all the sites are dubious to say the least. Like many henges, they appear as circular or near circular cropmarks on aerial photographs. Characteristic cropmarks have been identified in fields at Whitehouse Farm, Clifford; Stowe Farm, Whitney-on-Wye; Upper Chilstone House, Madley and Brandon Camp, Adforton.

Unfortunately this kind of evidence is ambiguous and interpretation can be a fairly hazardous business. It is quite possible that the cropmarks do not represent the remains of henges but of some other kind of site—they may be ploughed out barrows or they may be ring ditches. It is argued that the latter, which are generally considered to have been constructed slightly later than henges, were used as focal points in the landscape, as meeting places sited on neutral territory where two or more groups could come together to exchange gifts—though they may have had a ceremonial purpose.

Monuments which almost certainly had a ritual function are stone circles. These simple yet intriguing monuments tend to capture the popular imagination—it is easy to imagine the Bronze Age shaman conducting mysterious rituals within the stones. We cannot pretend to know the precise nature of these ceremonies, but stone circles may represent a new system of belief in which the sun and moon were the main objects of worship. Many archaeologists go further, suggesting that stone circles served as prehistoric observatories. A single unprepossessing example can be found in Herefordshire at Longtown, at the end of a long climb to the top of Loxidge Tump on the Black Mountains.

The Early Bronze Age, however, was not an era of peaceful change—the new aristocracy had to fight their way to the top. At Crickley Hill in Gloucestershire, hundreds of leaf-shaped arrowheads offer fairly convincing evidence that open warfare was rife.

Once power had been attained, perhaps by defeating neighbours in war and seizing their lands, an aspiring chief had to retain his control—and this is where metal played a key role. The prestige he

Wern Perris standing stone, Michaelchurch Escley

45

gained as a successful war-leader could be enhanced by the trappings of success. In later days this would become the crown of the kingdom, but in Bronze Age society high quality bronze weaponry, gold and to a lesser extent amber symbolised legitimate power, as did the adoption of exotic practices such as beaker burials. Wealth and the use of foreign ideas were a confirmation of high social status, and made an essentially exploitative social order based upon the concentration of agricultural land in the hands of the few seem natural and immutable. A religious or ritual role, in addition to that of the chief, may have further strengthened the individual leader's position by making it appear that his authority was ordained by the gods. In such a way, hereditary Early Bronze Age aristocracies, supported by tribute paid for the use of their land by farmers, may have emerged.

Some of this tribute would undoubtedly have been redistributed among the chieftain's people in the form of feasts. Such lavish displays of 'generosity', which have been observed by anthropologists in Amazonia, along the northwest coast of North America and in Papua New Guinea, would have helped to minimise social unrest. Feasting would also have helped chieftains to establish marriage alliances, thereby consolidating local aristocracies.

As time went on, increasingly marginal soils—those over 300 metres above sea level—came under the plough. Early Bronze Age monuments located at very high elevations may indicate seasonal occupation and use of the highest land. In addition the pollen record shows that after about 1700 BC woodland clearance intensified and land was divided up into fields, indicating increasing concern with land ownership and allocation.

As a result of agricultural expansion, more and more tribute in the form of food and possibly textiles would have been channelled towards the centre of the local system, increasing the prosperity of the chief and enabling him to exchange gifts over an ever widening area, and to commission work from leading bronze-smiths in the 'international' style emanating from the Continent. This would have further enhanced his own prestige and that of the community over which he ruled.

Towards the end of the beaker period another change in burial practice occurred. Rather than individual inhumations under round

Beaker vessel from the Olchon Valley Cist Burial

barrows, the emphasis switched to cremation burials in level cemeteries. The dead became less visible than they had been in earlier
times, though often cremation cemeteries were positioned close to
earlier barrows, indicating continuity in the use of sites despite
changes in fashion. In Herefordshire, however, such continuity is
less apparent.

The most important burial sites of this period in Herefordshire
are located on the southern and eastern sides of the county—at
Mathon, near Colwall and Pontshill, near Ross-on-Wye, where a
finger-decorated cremation urn was found above a charcoal layer.
The cemetery at Southend Farm, Mathon was discovered during
sand quarrying operations in 1910. The remains of at least thirteen

*Contents of Olchon Cist Burial number 1, including Beaker vessel,
human remains and tanged and barbed arrowhead*

cremated individuals were found by the owner of the quarry, a Mr
Hodges. Some of these were partly surrounded and overlaid by
small, irregular flat stones, reflecting burial practice on the
Continent. In addition the site yielded several fragments of very

brittle cinerary urns, decorated with a line of bosses. The urns contained cremated human bone and were examined by the archaeologist Brigadier-general W.G. Hamilton.

Two of the urns were reconstructed and found to be bucket-shaped. Hamilton argued that they were comparable with examples belonging to the so-called Urnfield Culture of Continental Europe (also known as Halstatt A & B, for which see the Glossary), which spread as far south as Italy. An intrusion of Urnfield practices into Britain from the Lower Rhine had conventionally been dated to around 800 BC. However, the Mathon evidence seemed to push the spread of Urnfield influence back several centuries. Three of the interments were associated with bronze lance-heads dated to the Middle Bronze Age (1600-1000BC), as was a bronze disc, perhaps the central boss of a shield, and a stone battle-axe found slightly to the east of the main cemetery. These finds suggest that Herefordshire did not lag as far behind the Continent as previously thought.

In 1936, another fragmentary urn was found at Mathon, this time decorated with short diagonal incised markings, perhaps made by a fingernail. Hamilton suggested this was of a later type. But, the following year, a definite Middle Bronze Age urn came to light, corroborating the view that Continental ideas were quick to catch on. This example had an overhanging rim and a pattern of incised parallel lines, chevrons and dots. It was found about 35 metres north-east of the main cemetery.

It is not clear where the people who adopted the new ideas lived, though Hamilton suggested their settlements may have been on the Malvern Hills, just over three kilometres to the east and 'affording ample grazing ground and probably some cultivation'. Whether this was the case or not, they seem to have had quite wide-ranging contacts, for two flint flakes found in the sandpit were imported from sources at least fifty miles distant.

What has been written so far suggests that the entire body of Bronze Age evidence for Herefordshire is connected with death and the rituals surrounding death. Whilst this emphasis does reflect the sparseness of material from Bronze Age settlements, such evidence is not entirely lacking.

In 1946, local archaeologist and Woolhope Club member R. S. Gavin Robinson investigated a number of flint scatters which had appeared as a result of ploughing high on Cefn Hill, near Craswall. According to Gavin Robinson, these scatters represented 'living-floors'—perhaps the floors of huts of which traces had long since disappeared. Here, flint and later, as flint supplies dried up, shale and chert from Radnorshire, were worked up into implements such as knives, borers and scrapers.

The majority of these scatters were of Neolithic date, Gavin Robinson argued. But one, his Site C, just to the west of the Hay to Michaelchurch road, yielded two arrows of definite Bronze Age type. Furthermore, near a length of what may have been pre-historic dry-stone walling, he discovered some flints which showed signs of the coarse chipping technique typical of Bronze Age workmanship.

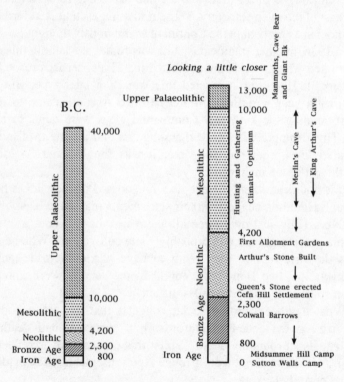

Herefordshire Time-Line:
The Prehistoric Phase

Clearly, Bronze Age Herefordians shared with their Neolithic forebears a predilection for 'high' living. Evidence from Cefn Hill goes some way to support the theory that Bronze Age people were gradually extending their farming activities into upland areas. However, the settlement was not new. It had been founded during the Neolithic period and suggests equally that the social and political disruption that occurred as the age of stone yielded to the age of metal did not prevent a degree of continuity between the two ages.

From about 1500 BC, as changes in the treatment of the dead became established, instability seems to have entered the Bronze Age social system, probably due, unlike the Neolithic to Bronze Age transition, to environmental rather than social and political factors. From the end of the last Ice Age 10,000 years ago, the climate of Europe went through a succession of dry and wet phases. These changes affected human society because they influenced the kinds of plants and animals available. For example, following the open grassland habitats of the Ice Age, the spread of woodland brought new animal species—and new food sources such as roe deer, red deer and wild boar—to Britain.

By the beginning of the Bronze Age—some 6,500 years later—the climate was relatively warm and dry and the vegetation was dominated by oak and alder woodland. It was a climate well suited to the spread of cereal cultivation. Commencing some time during the Middle Bronze Age (1600—1000 BC), however, the weather became increasingly cool and wet. This climatic shift would have made the upland farms colonised a few centuries earlier untenable. There would have been insufficient summer warmth to ripen wheat and barley crops, while excessive rainfall would have led to the over-development of plants and weakening of the straw. Furthermore, the high rainfall would have caused the formation of blanket bog in upland areas such as the Marches, where the soils soon became barren and useless to farmers.

The social effects of this change were compounded because the population by about 1500 BC was much higher than it had been earlier. Clearly, there was a strain on food resources, a crisis which initiated two responses. Firstly, lowland areas such as the Thames Valley were newly exploited and secondly, more forest was cleared to make way for ploughland and pasture.

It seems the old elites, who by this time were probably an established aristocracy, weathered the early stages of the crisis. In Herefordshire, new bronze forms appear. One of these is the 'palstave', an unwieldy hourglass-shaped axe which may have been invented in north Wales, though was perhaps inspired by products from northern Germany. A group of such palstaves together with a number of spearheads was discovered at Kyre Park, south-east of Tenbury Wells. In addition, two palstaves were found at Vowchurch; and single finds came to light at Oldbury Camp, Much Marcle; Weston-under-Penyard; Tram Inn and Colwall.

However, from about 1200 BC a period of upheaval seems to have affected the whole of Europe. Around this time, the centralised society of Mycenae in the Aegean collapsed and the population reverted to the more dispersed settlement pattern typical of other parts of Europe. In some parts of Britain, the system of small fields which developed in the earlier Bronze Age was written over by new linear boundary ditches dividing the landscape afresh and creating 'ranches' supporting a cattle-herding economy.

Agricultural activity in Britain generally seems to have intensified at this time, with many more practical tools appearing—sickles, for example, and axes for forest clearance—as new areas of lowland came under the plough.

Thus bronze was no longer used exclusively for items of personal display, though prestige bronzes such as barbed spears were still produced. The increasing demand for utilitarian bronzes stimulated a revolution in metal-working, giving rise to new casting methods coupled with other manufacturing processes such as sheet-metal working. These new conditions of high demand combined with more efficient technology may have enabled the highly skilled bronze smiths—operating as independent entrepreneurs directly supplying an expanding market—to break down the old aristocratic control of bronze. Their activities may have led ultimately to the devaluation of both bronze and bronze-related prestige, in turn giving rise to conflict, as symbolic warfare with prestige goods among an established elite was translated into open and violent competition for power. Certainly weaponry and shields (the latter making use of the new sheet-metal techniques) became more conspicuous at this time.

Artifacts from the Bronze Age including 4 socketed axes, 2 stone axes, 2 tanged and barbed arrowheads and a knife or dagger

A partial solution for the old aristocracy may have been to periodically take quantities of bronze out of circulation in an attempt to restore the value of the metal. The evidence for this are the deposits or hoards of metalwork which have been unearthed and dated to this period. This practice is particularly evident along the margin of the western upland zone, an area including the Marches and which was probably suffering waterlogging as a result of increased rainfall. Here significant deposits of barbed spearheads have been found in springs, bogs and other watery places. The metalwork may have been hidden under the guise of ritual dedications to the gods, anticipating later Celtic belief in the existence of water deities.

Alternatively, the metalwork could have been buried for safety, as has happened regularly in times of stress and warfare.

After 900 BC, hilltop sites such as the Breiddin, Powys began to be occupied. The increased use of bronze for tools suggests that the limitations imposed upon agricultural expansion by the continuous poor climate were being overcome by clearing more forest and by utilising existing farmland more efficiently by practising more frequent cropping and allowing shorter fallow periods. However, a more complex and technologically intensive agriculture would have demanded a greater degree of social organisation. It is in this light, perhaps, that we should view the emergent hilltop centres which developed throughout the Late Bronze Age and into the Iron Age. It would seem that the 'chiefdoms' which emerged at the beginning of the Bronze Age had, by the end of the period, become compact political units with hill settlements at their centres.

Were the heads of these political units descendants of the Early Bronze Age elites? Some suggest that the increasing number of so-called Halstatt C swords in Late Bronze Age Britain—at a time when the native aristocracies had been weakened by conflict—indicates the arrival of Continental raiding parties who may have brought elements of early Celtic culture to these shores. However, Celtic traits are already visible in the archaeological record from around 1200 BC, and it is not necessary to look abroad for their origins. Finds of this period include bronze horse-bits and harness pieces, as well as a variety of fittings for wagons and chariots—all typical Celtic aristocratic trappings. The forms of these bronze objects are very similar to others found in northern France, and close links between the two areas may have led to actual migrations from Brittany across the Channel in the succeeding Iron Age. Conceivably, the old elites did survive the crises of climatic deterioration, inflation, competition and conflict, adapting to changed economic and social realities by evolving a new system of rural administration and new forms of prestige such as horse-riding and raiding.

With the Halstatt bronze, however, came iron and the death knell for the old prestige economy. Never again would bronze, which had done so much to promote the development of a hierarchical society in Britain and Europe, be used for tools and weapons.

Bush Bank Standing Stone

Small standing stone
Location: 3km north of Canon Pyon (SO 449 515)
Access: By the side of a minor road

From Canon Pyon on the A4110 (originally the southern section of Watling Street, the Roman Road to Kenchester) head north till you reach the hamlet of Bush Bank. Here, take the left turn just before the Bush public house, signposted to Kings Pyon. 100m down this lane is the standing stone, clearly visible on the left.

Very little is known about the origins of this standing stone, even whether or not it has prehistoric origins. In 1933, local archaeologist Alfred Watkins suggested that this stone could be part of a monolithic Wayside Cross which had been defaced during the Civil War. In addition, the stone has been removed to its present position in the recent historical past, possibly from an adjacent field. No other visible monuments are in close proximity. However, there is a round barrow at Canon Pyon, 2.5km to the south-west, and the Wergin's Stone lies 7km to the south-east. The spatial distribution of the two standing stones and barrow is very similar to the pairing of barrows and standing stones occurring in the west of the county, albeit in distances of kilometres rather than hundreds of metres.

The stone's shape and height at approximately 1.3m, are comparable to other standing stones in Herefordshire. If of Bronze Age date, a view which the authors hold, this is one of only a handful of Bronze Age monuments that are located this far east in the county; the others being the two round barrows on the Malvern Hills, close to the Shire Ditch, and the Bronze Age cemetery at Mathon.

The possible round barrow at Canon Pyon

Kinsham Standing Stone and Barrows

Two round barrows and a moved and 'dumped' standing stone
Location: 5km east of Presteigne (SO 358 641-4)
Access: By permission from nearby farm

From Presteigne, take the B4362 signposted to Leominster. Approximately 3km from Presteigne, take the left turn to Upper and Lower Kinsham. Drive for 2km. Just before the village of Lower Kinsham and on the left-hand side is a driveway to New House Farm. Permission is required at this farm in order to visit the standing stone and barrows. From the farm drive entrance, walk towards the village. Immediately on the right, past the first house (a 'black and white' cottage) is a small gate to a paddock. Walk south to the next gate and meadow beyond. Continue south, keeping left to the edge of this large and often wet meadow. Kinsham Standing Stone can be clearly seen in the bottom corner of this meadow.

Probably transported during the last glacial period by the ice, the stone when standing measured over 2.7m high, and was one of the tallest standing stones in Herefordshire. Sadly, in the recent past the Devil Stone (as it is known locally) has been moved and 'dumped' in its present position. Its original location was probably equidistant between the two barrows. On the underside of the stone are believed to be seven cupmarks, but because the stone has remained in this position for many years, the exact location and pattern of these marks is not known. Visible on the top side of the stone is a group of linear gouges which are probably recent additions.

In association with the stone are two Bronze Age round barrows. Both are within a few hundred metres either side of the stone. The best preserved of the two lies close to the River Lugg, about 100m west of the stone. The second, 300m to the south-east, has been ploughed up and is now part of a modern field boundary. Bronze Age monuments are often grouped this way throughout Herefordshire and there is a similar pattern at Comb, 2km west of Kinsham.

Very few ideas have been put forward to explain the location of such monuments, or the significance of the groupings. As stated in the main text, barrows are always constructed either on the tops of hills or in valley bottoms. We would suggest that those located in river meadows post-date those on hills though probably, in general, not by many years, for we now know that the Bronze Age was a period of rapid and dramatic change.

Although the dating of standing stones is difficult, the relationship of the Kinsham one with the barrows is suggestive of a similar date.

Longtown Cairn and Stone Circle

> Bronze Age cairn
> Location: 3km west of Longtown, on top of the
> Black Mountains (SO 300 283)
> Access: From a public path

At the northern end of Longtown village, turn left on the narrow road signposted Mountain Road. Proceed along this road for approximately 2.3km to Upper Turant Farm. 50m past this farm is a sharp right-hand bend and further on a gated road and cattle-grid. You must park near here. From the cattle-grid, take the left track up the mountain. When climbing up, keep the mountain road from Longtown directly in line with the mountain. The cairn and stone circle can be clearly seen at the summit (560m above sea level). Please note that the track to the summit is very steep, and the weather may be changeable!

From these two monuments there are outstanding views across the whole of Herefordshire. The Malverns can be seen 50km to the east. Directly below lies the Olchon Valley where, in the 1930s, two Bronze Age cist burials were discovered. The cist burials and cairn and stone circle on the Black Mountains are, in our opinion, directly related.

The cairn and stone circle are approximately 30m from the Welsh border and Offa's Dyke Path. The centre of the cairn has, in the past, been excavated and therefore is recognisable by its doughnut shape. Small stones and locally quarried rock are clearly visible around the sides of the cairn. The stone circle is at present covered by undergrowth, and lies approximately 10m from the cairn. Use of the track that separates both monuments has eroded away the topsoil to reveal an ancient (Bronze Age and earlier) surface. Very little information exists about either of these monuments.

However, one can picture clan chieftains and the shaman using both for religious ceremonies, burial customs and possibly in astronomy. The reason for siting these and other Bronze Age monuments in upland areas could well be to allow the shamans to get closer to the heavens. Their location could even have acted as a halfway point between the known territory in the valleys, and the unknown of the skies and stars.

The Shire Ditch Barrows, Colwall

> A pair of Bronze Age round barrows
> Location: On top of the Malverns (SO 768 421)
> Access: From a public footpath leading either from the
> Herefordshire Beacon or from the Wyche Cutting

Possibly dating from the Early Bronze Age, both barrows have at one time been excavated, with their centres hollowed out, probably as a result of treasure hunting during the nineteenth century. The mound of the one barrow is oval-shaped (9m by 12m and 0.75m high) and was also damaged during the construction of the Shire Ditch during the thirteenth century. The ditch has revealed part of the barrow's stone construction. The more northerly barrow is 11m in diameter and stands 1m high and is also constructed of stone.

Although both barrows are visible from many points on top of the Malverns, they cannot be seen from lower down the slope or from the surrounding countryside—thus creating restricted visibility, a feature of many other upland barrows in the county.

The reason for this restricted visibility is unclear, though the authors suggest it may be that the barrows act not only as burial monuments, but also as either territorial markers or even symbolic places within the landscape. Previously, during the Neolithic, areas around chambered tombs may well have had access restricted to certain strata of society, and these restrictions may have been later adapted to exclude visitors to ritual or sacred areas around Early Bronze Age barrows.

The Queen's Stone

Vertically grooved standing stone
Location: 1km west of Goodrich (SO 562 182)
Access: Permission required from nearby Huntsham Court

The Queen's Stone, probably one of the most curious standing stones in Herefordshire, lies in a large meadow in a loop of the River Wye, below Symonds Yat. In order to visit this monument, permission must be obtained from the owners of nearby Huntsham Court—approximately 1km south of Huntsham Bridge. From the village of Goodrich proceed south for 500m and turn left over Huntsham Bridge. Carry on along the road to reach the Court, itself on the left.

To reach The Queen's Stone, return to the bridge and park. Walk west alongside the River Wye through two meadows for 600m. The Queen's Stone can be clearly seen in the second meadow. Known in Anglo-Saxon folklore as the Cwen Stan (The Woman's Stone), the Queen's Stone is believed by local people to have been moved to its present position in the late medieval period.

The stone is shaped from local sandstone conglomerate, and probably originates from nearby Huntsham Hill. It stands approximately 2m high and has a series of twelve vertical grooves, each groove being around 170mm deep. Also present on the eastern face is a single cupmark. Alfred Watkins conducted a small excavation in 1924 and found that the grooves stopped abruptly at the then ground level, though now they run some 25cm below ground. Watkins found the stone had a total height of 4.7m.

In 1934, Watkins gave a lecture to 500 members of the Wood-craft Folk in which he suggested that the Queen's Stone was a sacrificial stone where victims were placed in a wicker cage on top of the stone. The wicker structure would have been built up from poles inserted in the grooves. Though many others have concluded that the grooves result from erosion, the authors tend to think that they are deliberately carved, not for holding a sacrificial wicker cage, but merely as decoration, perhaps as with the Devil's Arrows at Boroughbridge and the Longstone at Stanton, in the Forest of Dean. The vertical direction of the grooves may be pointing to some earth deity, whilst the elongated shape of this and many other standing stones may symbolise a link between agriculture and the earth. Similar present day Christianised shrines dedicated to fertility and the earth are found in many southern Mediterranean countries.

The Queen's Stone is one of four monuments of Bronze Age date found in this area; there being three barrows inside the ramparts of Little Doward Camp, about 3km south-west of the Queen's Stone. In addition, many artifacts including polished stone and flint axes of Late Neolithic or Early Bronze Age date have been recovered from nearby English Newton, Huntsham Hill, St Weonards, Walford and Welsh Newton.

Wergin's Stone

Standing stone set in a socket
Location: 2km north of Hereford (SO 530 439)
Access: 25m from a minor road

From Hereford, head along the A4103 towards Worcester. At the edge of the city take the second turn off the roundabout, signposted to Sutton St Nicholas. After about 1.5km on the right is a large river meadow (known since medieval times as the 'Wergins') in which the stone is clearly visible, some 25m from the road.

The stone itself is unworked and stands 1.8 metres high. It is set in a stone socket which is most probably a more recent addition. The stone socket is a square block and could well be a millstone dating from the post-medieval period.

This monument has been the subject of much debate. Some archaeologists (T.G.E. Powell *et al*) have argued that it originally formed part of a Neolithic Tomb, perhaps an upright support. The authors are unhappy with this theory because virtually nothing of Neolithic date exists nearby. If anything, the stone dates from the Bronze Age, although even this suggestion is rather tenuous given the fact that there is very little other evidence within the locality. The nearest Bronze Age monuments are Bush Bank Standing Stone and a round barrow at Canon Pyon, both lie approximately 7km NNW of the Wergin's Stone. Unfortunately, these two monuments also have questionable origins. Bush Bank Standing Stone has at some time within the recent past been relocated, probably from a nearby field, whilst Canon Pyon Round Barrow may well be an early medieval castle motte—the site has never been excavated. But if all three monuments are from the Bronze Age, then there is the possibility that they could represent territorial markers. Similar Bronze Age clusters exist throughout the county, especially in the west. Also worth considering is that this area has been intensively farmed over the past 2,000 years, and therefore other monuments may have been destroyed under the plough.

The Wergin's Stone also has an historical past. It is believed that it was a meeting place for, according to Ella Mary Leather (1912), the 'ceremonious collection of an annual money payment', probably between neighbouring parishes. In 1652, the stone was moved 'twelve score paces' (or 'two hundred and forty paces') in order to mark the spot where three parish boundaries meet. Legend has it that the stone, also known as the Devil's Stone, was moved by supernatural agencies during the mid-seventeenth century. This story obviously contradicts the earlier, more probable account.

The Iron Age

The landscape of Neolithic (or New Stone Age, 4200-2300 BC) Herefordshire had been dominated by memorials to the dead. Over very long periods of time, austere communal tombs such as Arthur's Stone and Cross Lodge Barrow, which could be opened and re-opened, served as repositories for the dead, periodically interred en masse by the light of ceremonial fires and accompanied by gifts of food, pottery and weapons. Unlike our own Christian graveyards, there was no commemoration of individual life in these monuments: an individual was lost among the bones of his or her ancestors.

During the Late Neolithic and Early Bronze Age (2500-2000 BC), the old obsession with dead ancestors seems to have waned. Some argue that new people arrived in Britain from the Rhineland. Certainly, society began to change, for powerful chiefs belonging to a fashion-conscious nouveau riche appear in the archaeological record, buried with their treasured possessions in individual graves under round barrows. This new individualism marks a complete break with the corporate mentality of earlier times.

A thousand years and more later, these early chiefdoms had become distinct political units headed by a horse-riding aristocracy. In their wake came a new desire to celebrate living communities rather than dead ones.

Neolithic and Bronze Age (2500-800 BC) settlements are, by and large, invisible to us today. Compared with the work that went into building their tombs, these people seem to have invested little time and effort into constructing houses and villages to impress the eye.

By contrast, during the Iron Age (800 BC-AD 48) people, equipped only with weighted digging sticks and antler picks, wicker baskets and the shoulder-blades of oxen, poured enormous effort into creating massive walled settlements.

Standing high above the surrounding countryside upon prominent hilltops, these structures—the larger ones representing about 30,000 man-hours of effort—would have signalled to the outside world for miles around that this was the home of a powerful, secure and thriving community. So solid and permanent were these earth-walled enclosures that they have survived for over two-and-a-half thousand years to the present day. Now eroded and often tree-covered, they bear the signs of extreme antiquity. Nevertheless, breaking the skyline with ramparts which still sometimes stand to a height of five metres or more they remain striking monuments, every bit as impressive as the ruined Marcher castles of a later age. Well over fifty of these hill-top earthworks are known in Herefordshire and are part of an extensive zone of Iron Age forti-fied settlements which stretches from north-west Wales, through the Marches and the Cotswolds to Wessex in the south of England.

Later generations marvelled at these vast structures which seemed to belong to a world in which aggression and warfare were rife. Standing in majestic isolation, they tested the imagination of local people. Were they the work of Romans or Saxons—or did they have a supernatural origin? Credenhill Camp was believed to have been the stronghold of Creda, the first King of the Mercians, a sixth century Saxon ruler who is supposed to have entered Herefordshire in the 580s and driven out the older Romano-British population. It is said superstition prevented the Saxons from perma-nently occupying the old Roman towns. Instead they chose sites away from the old population centres—sites such as lofty Credenhill Camp, a gigantic 20-hectare settlement high above Roman Kenchester and close to a Roman road which crossed the River Wye. In other parts of Britain, similar structures were popu-larly thought of as sites once occupied by Alfred or Arthur. Alfred's Castle is a small earthwork in Oxfordshire, whilst South Cadbury Castle in Somerset is still held by many to be the site of Camelot.

With the growth of scientific archaeology in the twentieth century, these monuments, dubbed 'hillforts', became the focus of systematic investigation and were found to pre-date the Arthurian world by many centuries—though South Cadbury apparently was

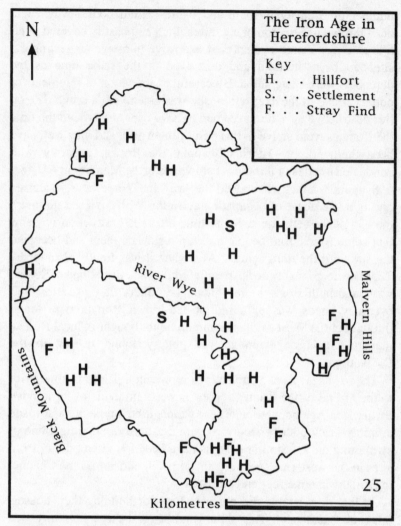

The Iron Age in Herefordshire

Key
H . . . Hillfort
S . . . Settlement
F . . . Stray Find

N

River Wye

Malvern Hills

Black Mountains

Kilometres

25

refortified at around the time Arthur is likely to have lived. In 1948, Kathleen Kenyon, a distinguished archaeologist who later excavated the famous near-Eastern site of Jericho, began the first of several seasons' work in Herefordshire. She chose to look at Sutton Walls, a hillfort which overlooks the Lugg Valley at Sutton St Nicholas and which had been intensively quarried for gravel during the war. Dame Kathleen unearthed the remains of a society which had met a very violent end. Below the walls she discovered a number of exclusively male and battle-scarred bodies which had been thrown unceremoniously into a ditch and hastily covered over. She also discovered evidence of extensive burning, suggesting the site had been attacked and destroyed at the same time as the defenders were slaughtered. By careful examination of fragments of pottery found in the excavation, she was able to put a rough date on this destructive episode. It seemed to have occurred around the time the Romans were active in this part of the world, and may well have been the work of Ostorius Scapula, the Roman governor who conducted a series of ferocious campaigns in the Marches in AD 48.

Scapula's attack, if indeed he was the perpetrator, occurred during a late phase of occupation at Sutton Walls, but did not mark the end of the settlement. Some time after the destruction it seems that some Romanised people took up residence there and occupied the site until the third century AD, when it was finally abandoned. These were probably local people who gradually adopted Roman ways and built stone-floored huts. The pottery they used for their everyday needs was of a red or red-brown Roman type found throughout the West Midlands and no doubt bought in local Roman markets. It is quite unlike the pottery found deeper in the excavation.

The lower levels at Sutton Walls represent a period of time prior to the arrival of the Roman forces and contain evidence of a much earlier Iron Age population. These people used a type of hand-made crumbly black pottery decorated with a pattern resembling a line of swimming ducks. Similar designs have been found on pottery from sites in the western Cotswolds, in Cornwall and across the Channel in Brittany and the Iberian Peninsula.

At that time people did not use stone for building their houses, but timber and mud. This should not suggest the community was poor, however. Indeed, by the standards of the day the people seem to have been affluent. Enormous numbers of animal bones found by archaeologists suggest the inhabitants kept large herds and were well fed. The presence of loom weights tell us that they wove cloth—and several antler cheek-pieces belonging to bridles suggest they were probably keen horsemen too. Skilled iron workers also plied their craft, leaving behind large quantities of iron slag from the manufacture of tools and weapons. Numerous fragments of these iron objects were discovered during the course of the Sutton Walls' excavation. Among the fragmentary iron pieces were two sickles, clear evidence that these people not only raised stock, but cultivated the land too, producing wheat and barley which they ground up in hand mills or 'querns', common finds on British Iron Age sites.

Duck-stamped pottery rims

The hillforts, then, were thriving centres of population when the Romans came to Britain. But who were the architects and builders—the bands of Iron Age men, women and probably children too who invested all that effort? According to the pottery evidence, the earlier settlers at Sutton Walls were related in some way to prehistoric communities in France, Spain and Portugal. Kathleen Kenyon believed that, at the time of the Roman conquest, they had been living in Herefordshire for about 150 years, but that their original homeland had been in northern France. She called them 'Iron Age B' people, successors to the Iron Age A folk who were the first iron users in Britain. The latter were roughly contemporary with Continental Halstatt C and D peoples who buried their dead under barrows accompanied by four-wheeled vehicles and from whom a knowledge of iron-working in Britain probably derived.

In the decades since Kenyon published her report, however, her dates have been revised and they are generally agreed to be much too recent. Using results obtained by radiocarbon dating, it is still possible to argue that the Sutton Walls people migrated from France, but this migration would have occurred before about 250

BC, perhaps as early as 390 BC. Why they decided to move we do not know. Kathleen Kenyon believed it was as a response to Roman aggression in Gaul, but with this more accurate date, Roman activity was something for future generations to worry about.

One alternative explanation is based on nature. We now believe that the Late Bronze Age and Early Iron Age (1200—700 BC) was a time of population increase and worsening climate. The weather became cooler and wetter over much of northern and western Europe and farming communities that had been able to earn a living from upland farms during the preceding Middle Bronze Age now found their farmland unproductive as increased rainfall encouraged peat growth and transformed fertile soil into sterile heathland. We know that Dartmoor was abandoned at this time, as were many upland areas which had previously been heavily populated. In Herefordshire it is likely that the same happened with the upland areas around the Golden Valley and Cefn Hill. The farmers moved down into the lowlands where they came into contact with communities already established in the river valleys. This, coupled with the fact that population levels were rising and were probably similar to or greater than those of the Middle Ages, gave rise to competition for land and may explain the need for prominent fortified settlements, statements of land ownership as much as defensive structures. An estimate for Herefordshire at the time of the Roman Conquest suggests that the population stood at around 33,000, or 15 people per square kilometre. This compares to a Domesday population estimated at some 20,000, or 9 people per square kilometre.

Perhaps the Sutton Walls people left Brittany because they were squeezed out by more powerful and land-hungry neighbours. The difficulty with this explanation is that the climatic change seems to have begun around 1200 BC or even earlier, more than half a millennium before our emigrants are supposed to have left France—were farming communities still feeling the effects in the third or fourth centuries BC? Other writers have suggested that the migration was part of a general pattern of aggressive tribal expansion across Europe in the early decades of the fourth century, which also took northern and central European tribes as far south as Italy.

Whatever the motive, or combination of motives, according to Kathleen Kenyon the continental immigrants, perhaps prehistoric refugees, landed on the Cornish coast. Here some settled. Others, however, moved on, following the coast and river valleys northwards. Settlements were founded at Bredon Hill on the western fringe of the Cotswolds and in the far west at Pen Dinas near Aberystwyth. The most northerly group followed the valleys of the Wye and Lugg as far as Sutton Walls, where they put down roots and established satellite settlements at Dinedor and Aconbury.

In these settlements generation succeeded generation, regulating their lives according to the perennial demands of the farming calendar. In spring, cows calved and ewes lambed. Surplus milk may have been turned into cheese by the villagers and stored for future use. At this time too, the draught cattle, which were descended ultimately from the large wild aurochs, but which by the Iron Age had been selectively bred to produce compact animals resembling the modern Dexter, were harnessed to the ploughs. Iron Age rock carvings from Scandinavia, southern France and northern Italy offer us a glimpse of the prehistoric farmer at work. They depict scenes of ploughmen following their cattle, which are harnessed in pairs to wooden ploughs. It seems these images served as fertility icons, encouraging the earth goddess to do her work, as the ploughmen are generally depicted with erect phalluses. Clearly primitive magic was a potent ingredient in the successful agricultural formula. A beneficent deity, impressed by the virility of the farmers in her care, could mean the difference between life and death for a prehistoric community. Actual examples of the ploughs used by these peoples have been recovered from peat bogs in Denmark and Scotland. How they came to be in the bogs in the first place is not always clear: perhaps they were thrown in as dedications to the gods; or perhaps they were simply abandoned by farmers when the climate deteriorated to such a point that the land was deserted.

The anaerobic conditions of such bogs have ensured the survival of materials such as wood and leather—and even, in some cases, human tissue—for thousands of years. Indeed, so well-preserved are these artifacts that archaeologists have been able to copy the methods used in the construction of ploughs and have built replicas which have proved to be highly efficient. The Iron Age plough differed from its modern equivalent in that it lacked a mould board and merely scratched the surface of the soil rather than turning it over in furrows. Consequently, fields needed to be ploughed in two directions, crossing each other, in order to break up the soil sufficiently for sowing. On slopes, the ploughing action caused soil to 'creep' downhill. Eventually, the accumulated earth at the foot of the slope would form a sizable bank or 'lynchet'. These features are still sometimes visible in the landscape delineating Iron Age field systems. A good example can be seen locally at the Breiddin, Powys, outside the entrance to the hillfort. Another possible example is visible below the promontory hillfort at Dorstone.

After ploughing and sowing, the next outburst of agricultural activity came at harvest-time. The ears of corn which had ripened over the summer months were cut from the stalks with iron sickles, of the type discovered at Sutton Walls, and brought to the village for cleaning and threshing. Once this process was complete, the grain was stored, either in pits or in granaries. It has been suggested that as many as a half of all the rectangular structures discovered at Croft Ambrey were grain stores. These granaries may have had raised floors to allow air to circulate beneath the building, and been generally similar in design to granaries found in farmyards all over Europe until recent years.

Threshing and cleaning also produced waste, such as husks, which could be used as animal feed. Following the harvest, the livestock would be brought in from the upland pastures and river meadows and allowed to forage in the stubble fields. Cattle, sheep and pigs (whose rooting activities broke up the soil) could all glean something from the harvested fields, and their manure helped to restore the fertility to the soil.

Around the margins of the cultivated land lay thick tracts of oak, elm and hazel wildwood. Although the trend was towards forest clearance and the creation of a predominantly open landscape, woodland continued to offer a vital resource to Iron Age communities, and some of it seems to have been carefully managed by coppicing. The forest, as well as having a sacred significance, was a source of fuel, both for domestic and industrial uses (such as iron smelting). It also provided a supply of building materials for houses, granaries and fences. For huts and grain stores, close-grained oak was generally preferred and was obtained from 45-60 year old trees. In addition to wood, Iron Age communities gleaned another very important product from the forest. This was winter fodder for cattle and sheep. In summer, farmers and their families went out into the forest to gather twigs and small branches from elm and ash trees. These were bundled together and laid on specially designed drying racks until the summer sun turned the leaves into a highly palatable food which could be stored for the winter, just like hay. The practice seems to be as old as farming itself in Europe, dating back to the Neolithic period, and is not unknown today.

Season upon season, year upon year, the finely balanced cycle continued. When the Romans arrived and disrupted this age-old system, some believe they called the hillfort-dwellers of Herefordshire the 'Silures', one of a host of prehistoric British tribes possessing extensive territories at the time of the Roman Conquest. The Roman chroniclers have left us a vivid picture of the unruly tribesmen their armies struggled to subdue, a picture somewhat at odds with the bucolic portrait just presented. To the eyes of the civilised writers from the south, the Silures were a very wild bunch indeed, and rather odd-looking too. They did not have the fair skins typical of northern Europeans, but were dark-skinned and curly-haired. They were also impetuous and unwilling to yield to the might of Rome. 'Praecipua Silurum pervicacia': 'the extraordinary stubbornness of the Silures!' Scapula must surely have had his work cut out when he started his campaign.

It seems that the lands of the Silures stretched far to the west, taking in Brecon, Radnor and much of south Wales. Some doubt exists as to whether they incorporated Herefordshire. However it has been the traditional antiquarian view—and the view we shall hold here—that they did, although tribal boundaries were probably quite fluid and dependent upon shifting political alliances and patterns of domination. Lying at the eastern extreme of Silurean territory, Hereford may at times have come within other spheres of influence: those of the Dobunnii based in Gloucestershire and the Cornovii of Shropshire. Other archaeologists, notably Dr Stanley Stanford, the excavator of Croft Ambrey and Credenhill, have argued that it was the Deceangi, conventionally thought of as occupying tribal lands in Flintshire, north Wales, who held sway over this part of the Marches. Whether Deceangi or Silures, we also know these ancient Herefordians as Celts, a widespread European people who, under the leadership of an aristocratic warrior class, shocked the 'civilised' Romans with scenes of human sacrifice and terrified them on the battlefield with wild dancing and shrieks of abuse. Woad-smeared and often naked, the Celtic warriors sped into battle in war chariots, hurling javelins before dismounting and laying into their foe with slashing swords. One classical authority informs us that the Celts in battle were very like the ancient Greek heroes of the Trojan Wars.

In common with the seventeenth and eighteenth century European explorers and colonists who opened up the New World and met for the first time the painted, tattooed and semi-naked tribesmen of woods and plains, the Roman legions encountered many exotic tribes as they pushed the frontier of their empire northwards across the mysterious forested lands of the Celts. Arverni, Aedui, Helvetii, Durotrigres...their names are numerous. Like the North (and South) American native peoples these societies had evolved over many thousands of years but had never developed the centralised authority to unite the various tribes, which thus tended to be in conflict with one another for most of the time. In spite of this, these Celtic peoples achieved notable military successes: in 390 BC, a time of tribal expansion, they attacked Rome itself; and in 279 BC were bold enough to enter Macedonia, where they suffered their first heavy defeat. So high was their reputation as fearless warriors that Hannibal used them as mercenaries, though he remained very wary of their 'treacherous' nature!

The picture of a disorganised, undisciplined and internecine society of warring aristocrats was changing fast in Celtic areas affected by the expanding influence of the Classical world, with the first signs of town-like settlement, industrial production, coinage and literacy appearing from central France to the Black Sea. But, over much of temperate Europe, Celtic society was quite unlike the Roman city-state, which by the fourth century BC had shaken off Etruscan influence to become the head of a political confederacy embracing the whole of the Italian peninsula. This political structure formed the basis of the Roman Empire, which was eventually to absorb most of the Celtic world. (Ireland was one part of this

74

Aerial view of Bach Hillfort

world untouched by Roman influence. Here prehistoric Celtic society continued largely unchanged until the Christian missionaries arrived in early medieval times. Christian scribes wrote down the oral hero-tales of ancient Ireland which offer us a tantalising portrait of what prehistoric Iron Age society may have been like over much of Europe).

Of the Celtic tribes encountered by the Romans, the Silures were among the most remote, inhabiting the misty fringes of the known world in the lands which the Greeks called 'hyperborean'—beyond the North Wind. The earliest Greek ethnographers and geographers, lacking much real knowledge of the peoples of northern Europe, had created an almost mythical race of peaceful vegetarians ruled by philosopher-kings or 'druids'. It was a confused picture based upon a dim perception of the actual Celtic or Iron Age societies of northern France and Britain—remote in geographical terms certainly, but nevertheless an integral part of a pan-European, iron-using culture which extended from the Carpathian Mountains and Asia Minor (St Paul refers to the 'foolish Galatians' of Asia Minor, a branch of Celtic society) to the shores of the Atlantic. Well over two thousand years before the idea of a European Community began to form in the minds of twentieth century politicians and businessmen, Celtic peoples traded freely with each other over wide areas and shared a common Indo-European language which was closely related to other languages of the ancient world—Latin, Greek and Sanskrit—and ancestral to Welsh, Irish, Gaelic and Breton.

The Celts also shared a reverence for the oak and for certain forest groves; for wells, springs, pools and the sources of rivers, many of which, such as the Wye and the Lugg, still bear their original names, though today the meanings are very uncertain. Sometimes votive deposits of metalwork and other objects were placed in the waters as dedications to the gods. Occasionally, artificial features served the same purpose. Thus ritual pits and shafts, in some cases over 100 feet deep, have been found by archaeologists to contain, among other things, pottery and human bones. One such shaft was discovered at Wapley, a hillfort near Staunton-on-Arrow. Like the other examples, this was probably regarded as an entrance to the underworld.

Stone temples only appear in the Celtic world during the Roman period. No doubt temple structures did exist earlier, but were, like Celtic houses, built of perishable materials which have not survived. In many cases they were probably built in forest clearings. Sometimes, however, sacred areas are found inside hillforts, a good example being the small enclosure containing significant quantities of broken pottery, animal bone and charcoal—perhaps the remains of some form of ritual—which was discovered at Croft Ambrey. This again has been dated to the Romano-British period, around AD 75, when the site was no longer a functioning Iron Age settlement. In these sacred places—forest groves, still and flowing water, sacred enclosures—the druids probably dabbled more in primitive magic than in philosophy as understood by the Greek world. Like the witch-doctors and shamans of aboriginal America, Siberia and parts of Africa, the chief druid of the King of Ireland apparently wore a bull's hide and a speckled bird head-dress. Similar figures, clad in animal skins, have been identified in European cave art of the Ice Age. In his bizarre get-up, the druid probably entered a trance-like state, helped on his way by hallucinogenic fungi, and performed sacrificial rituals to propitiate the fickle deities of the Celts. These included a horned god, who, according to a single Celtic inscription from Paris, was called Cernunnos; a warrior god, known by various names and possessing various attributes; and an archaic nature goddess, bringer of fertility and guardian of herds and flocks. According to the Romans, druidic rituals occasionally involved the shedding of human blood.

Of particular interest to archaeologists are the things these people made and used; their material culture. In the Iron Age, which embraces the period from about 800 BC to the Roman conquest and during which Celtic society took shape, this material culture consisted, unsurprisingly enough, of iron tools and weapons as well as fine pottery and a sophisticated and intricate art style found over large areas in the form of brooches and as decoration on shields, scabbards and many other items. Among the metal artifacts were the long sword and javelin, used to such devastating effect by the Celtic warrior, and the iron plough share, used with equal skill by the Celtic farmer. A 0.5m long iron sword with a broken tip, very similar to an example from Maiden Castle in Dorset, was found lying hilt-down at Croft Ambrey. Javelin heads were also discovered there and at Sutton Walls. During the latter centuries of this period, between about 400 BC and 250 BC, the time when the Sutton Walls Iron Age B people may have arrived, this material culture assumed its most characteristically Celtic appearance and is known as La Téne (The Shallows) after a lake site in Switzerland where a great ritual deposit of metalwork was discovered. A typical early La Téne bronze brooch, corroded and broken, but still recognisable, was discovered in the quarry area at Sutton Walls.

Structures are as much a part of a people's material culture as swords, pots and ploughshares. From Britain through central and northern France, Germany and Switzerland to Bohemia, the hillfort is a characteristic Celtic settlement type, though its form, and probably its function, varied over this wide area. In Britain, hillforts were concentrated in a broad arc extending from north-west Wales through the Marches and Cotswolds to the south coast. Herefordshire, then, lay towards the north-western extremity of hillfort distribution, out on a limb in relation to the rest of Europe. How unlike the noble philosophising savages of Greek ethnography the inhabitants of our sites must have been! A little behind the times by Celtic standards generally, the Silures, compared with their Continental cousins, showed only the merest signs of developing anything resembling towns—the hillforts themselves. Here on the periphery of the Celtic world the clan rather than the tribe was the main focus of loyalty for the individual Celt (the word actually derives from the Gaelic 'clann' meaning 'kindred group'). It was

77

the extended family into which he or she was born and it incorporated all those who believed they shared a common ancestor. A few in each clan may have been able to trace a direct link back to the founder, even though that founder may have been mythical rather than actual. These would have comprised the noble lineage, the upper stratum of a three-tier society. Below them were the farmers, who tilled their small fields and raised livestock; and the craftsmen, who fashioned both the items which made everyday life possible and the luxury goods prized by their superiors. At the bottom of the pile were the unfree workers who toiled virtually as slaves and may have been war captives, outside the clan system altogether.

The leaders of these extended kinship groups formed a warrior elite: arrogant and volatile, they shared a love of feasting and a penchant for head-hunting. More often than not they were—quite literally—at each other's throats, proving their worth as leaders by raiding neighbouring clans and making off with their property—most likely cattle, which are still an important form of wealth in many parts of the world today. We might imagine the triumphant warrior returning to his village on horseback following a successful raid, the heads of his victims tied to his saddle. After the stolen cattle had been corralled, the heads, prized by the warrior more highly than gold, were embalmed in cedar oil and impaled on stakes set up outside his hut for all to see and admire. A group of skulls treated in this way was actually discovered by archaeologists excavating the Iron Age site at Bredon Hill in Worcestershire—grisly confirmation of a practice attested by the Romans. In fact the Romans did the same thing themselves, though for different reasons.

Equally, the heads may have been deposited in a sacred place—a grove, ritual shaft or local shrine or temple—for the severed human head was a very potent religious symbol in the Celtic world, expressing the concept of divinity and the mysterious powers of the underworld. The Celts, however, merely adopted and adapted it, for the human head was already an ancient symbol in European society before Celtic peoples gave it their own particular significance. The Roman historian Livy tells us that the Celts adorned the skulls of their enemies with precious stones and used them as vessels for holy water in ceremonies involving ritual drinking. Skulls have usually been found at the bottom of wells and shafts, often accompanied by pottery and other artifacts. And Celtic artists sculpted images of the human head in wood, stone and bronze. Caesar described some of these as 'uncouth', hewn by axe from an untrimmed tree trunk. Five thousand such wooden images were found in a single deposit at a spring in the Auvergne. At Long Wittenham, in Berkshire, sculpted heads came to light inside a rectangular ritual earthwork.

Once inside the sacred realm, the trophies would have become the preserve of the druids, who were responsible for the ritual aspect of Celtic society. It was they who were the repositories of traditional wisdom—'the Magi of the Gauls and Britons' as Pliny romantically describes them—and acted as intermediaries between this world and the next. The Druids taught of the continuity of a warrior's life beyond the grave, a belief which inspired him to reckless bravery and to have with him in his grave all the necessities for fighting, feasting and arrogant self-display in the next world. To this end, aristocratic Celtic graves were regarded, like the ritual shafts, pits and wells, as entrances to the underworld and contained two-wheeled chariots in which the dead warrior was laid out, along with various pieces of horse-gear. One of the most famous graves was discovered at La Gorge Meillet in the Marne region of France in 1876. Such burials are less common in Britain than on the Continent, but there is an important burial group on Humberside, the latest of which was discovered at Garton Slack in 1984. No doubt much elaborate ritual surrounded these interments, which were afterwards covered by a burial mound. Sometimes, it seems, burial mounds remained important sites in the cultural life of the Celtic community, as focal points for clan gatherings and the performance of ritual. No such Iron Age burial mounds have been found in Herefordshire (but see the entry for Poston Camp and a possible associated mound), although some mounds that have been assigned to the Bronze Age may in fact be of Iron Age date—so few have been excavated that it is difficult to say categorically that they belong to one period rather than another.

The druids themselves seem to have been most active in Britain and parts of France, where they were accorded high social status. But they remain shadowy figures. The only first hand description of them is found in an account of Paulinus' attack on Anglesey in AD

61, where they are portrayed as howling priests inhabiting blood-stained groves. The clinical white-robed figures of modern myth seem a far cry from this chilling image, a romantic creation of recent centuries rather than accurate representations of an ancient priesthood. It is unlikely we shall ever have a true picture of these enigmatic figures.

We have seen that Celtic society was brutally competitive at the top. Those who competed successfully enjoyed high status and access to exotic trade items such as fine pottery and Mediterranean wine, for which they probably exchanged typical British commodities such as slaves, hunting dogs, woollen textiles and metals via middlemen operating in southern France. Possession of exotic goods would have further enhanced their standing in society, for it meant they were able to be more lavish in feast-giving. A popular leader—'high-spirited and quick to fight', as the Greek writer Strabo tells us—could command a large following: but to maintain it he had to keep on proving himself, looking further afield for new challenges.

The Romans tell us of one such leader among the Silures. His name has various forms: Caractacus in Latin, he would have been called Caratacos in his native tongue and is sometimes known as Caradoc today. In the folk-lore of Herefordshire he is portrayed as a local champion of the Celts, standing against the might of Rome. So successful was Caratacos in the competition for prestige and influence that when the Roman legions met him he was leader of the whole Silurian nation, which must have numbered tens of thousands at that time. Perhaps the very large hillfort at Credenhill—at 20 hectares the largest in the area—was his capital. Presumably, Caratacos' wealth in cattle was great, for, to have attained the status of paramount chief of the Silures, he must have raided and reduced to the status of vassal a large number of formerly independent clan chiefs. We must not, however, forget an important factor in Caratacos' rise to power—the coming of Rome. This event heralded a period of massive upheaval in many parts of Britain and the beginning of the violent end for Celtic society, as the evidence from Sutton Walls makes graphically clear. Homes were burned: entire communities were eradicated and dispersed. The research of anthropologists who have studied the effects of the clash between colonial power and clan-based society in other parts of the world sheds light upon the social and political processes which may have given rise to a figure such as Caratacos. They have questioned the use of the word 'tribe', a label which we have used liberally in this book, arguing that the tribe is essentially a creation of colonial influence: a 'response to invasion or domination by a state-organised society.' The Roman invasion of Britain was just such an event, a 'national emergency' during which inter-clan rivalries would have had to be buried for the time being and a larger Celtic identity assumed. In such a crisis, a leader of extraordinary qualities, be it man or woman, such as Boudicca of the Iceni, would have been needed, with the political and military skills to weld the clans into a single tribal entity under their own paramount leadership. Caratacos was one such charismatic leader, a successful guerrilla fighter who gave the Romans determined resistance and managed to elude the shackles of Ostorius Scapula for several years before being taken in chains to Rome. Had the invasion never occurred, there would have been little scope for Caratacos to display his leadership abilities and he may well have remained just another small-time chieftain engaged in petty tit-for-tat raiding with his nearest neighbours.

Prior to the coming of the Romans, therefore, Celtic territories were probably much smaller than the extensive 'tribal' lands identified above, consisting perhaps of no more than a hillfort and its agricultural hinterland. These territories probably belonged to individual clans, among whom raiding was endemic and the normal means of inter-community contact.

The territories do not seem to have been of equal size. The larger ones—with hillforts of 8 hectares or more—lay in the central zone of the future county, an area of fertile lowland with occasional low hills and proximity to water. Another group of medium to large hillforts lies on the western fringe of Herefordshire and may reflect an economy with an emphasis on pastoralism and the grazing of herds and flocks on higher pastures. (See Appendix 1).

It is possible that the hillforts themselves were the residences of these small-time chiefs and their noble kinsmen, the walls affording protection to the ruling elite, as well as being unambiguous symbols of power, clearly visible reminders to those who toiled in the fields below of the prevailing power structure. It is an attractive interpretation, but one which is hard to reconcile with the evidence. In general, the hillforts contain little to suggest they were the seats of a ruling minority, indeed little to suggest they were anything but the homes of relatively affluent farmers and craftspeople.

Those who actually worked the land, however, may have lived outside the walls of the hillforts in small farmsteads. Although only two Iron Age farmsteads are proven in Herefordshire—at Kenchester and Wellington Quarry—many more are known in Worcestershire, and it is probable that further archaeological work in this county will reveal more evidence of lowland settlement. As well as supporting themselves and their immediate families, the Iron Age farmers may have also supplied the hillfort-dwellers with food, perhaps in exchange for the implements and utensils they needed to carry on their daily lives.

In addition to being craftspeople, the hillfort-dwellers may have overseen agricultural production, rather than engaging directly in the work themselves. It has been suggested that British hillforts were principally secure food stores. Certainly over half of the structures in those intensively excavated seem to have been granaries. The hillforts may have served as central places in the local economy, with harvested grain being brought inside the walls for threshing, cleaning and storage. Cattle may have also been brought there for corralling following a successful raid, and sheep for lambing, shearing and slaughter.

Perhaps the hillfort-dwellers co-ordinated these activities as an administrative class between the peasant farmers and the nobles. They may have redistributed the stored food among the community on the basis of need, while channelling tribute up the social scale to the aristocracy, who may or may not have lived in the hillforts.

It is tempting to go a stage further and suggest that the hillforts were in the process of evolving into towns. In common with a medieval urban settlement such as Hereford, the hillforts possessed defences, planned street layouts—apparent at Croft Ambrey, Credenhill Camp, Midsummer Hill and Herefordshire Beacon—and large populations, perhaps as high as 4,000 at Credenhill Camp. Furthermore, they may have been home to an administrative class and seem definitely to have supported craft specialists.

However, towns are continuously occupied places. The lack of a permanent water supply at many of Herefordshire's hillforts suggests strongly that they were principally secure storage and redistributive centres, with perhaps seasonal, rather than permanent, occupation. Furthermore, at only two sites—Croft Ambrey and Wapley—is there any trace of organised religion, another feature of urban settlement. Moreover, the evidence for religious activity at Croft Ambrey dates from the Romano-British period, when the site had ceased to be a functioning settlement. And at none of the sites is there any evidence at all for the minting and use of coinage in the Iron Age. Iron Age coins that have come to light in the county have been stray finds, often discovered in areas of Roman activity, though a sword-shaped iron currency bar was discovered at Croft Ambrey. The latter became common in southern Britain during the second and first centuries BC and probably represent a medium of barter. It should be emphasised that further south—and especially on the Continent—there are strong indications that the hillforts were evolving rapidly into urban settlements towards the end of the first millennium. These were known to the Romans as 'oppida'. In Herefordshire, however, the precise nature of the hillfort remains a mystery.

They seem to have arisen due to increasing population and the resultant pressures this brought. In such circumstances we might imagine that clan loyalties, which had perhaps been rather nebulous in the Bronze Age, intensified. As rights in land became more critical, territories became more sharply defined and conflict more prevalent. Conceivably, near the centre of these clan territories, the prehistoric engineers and labourers designed and constructed large strongholds high above the surrounding land as clear territorial markers and secure stores for vital food supplies—which may also have acted as safe havens for lowland farmers subject to the depredations of neighbouring clans.

As for the antiquity of the county's hillforts, much activity seems to have occurred between about 400 and 250 BC, perhaps as Iron Age B influence spread into the area. However, since Kathleen Kenyon's day, further archaeological research into the Iron Age has been carried out in Herefordshire, particularly on hillforts. Dr Stanford, then of Birmingham University, led a major excavation at

Croft Ambrey in the sixties. Similar excavations were carried out elsewhere in Britain, and all benefited from the relatively new technique of radiocarbon dating. Stanford's results indicated that Croft Ambrey was older than had been thought and was contemporary with other large, well-defended hillforts such as Danebury in Wessex and the Heuneberg on the Upper Danube. While Stanford found much evidence to suggest that there had been a phase of redesign and enlargement at the site around 390 BC, it seems work started on the first defences around 550 BC. Furthermore, the settlement within the walls was of quite a different type to that of later hillforts such as Sutton Walls. Square buildings were laid out with barrack-like uniformity over the whole of the interior; whereas at Sutton Walls rectangular buildings seem to have been concentrated at the rear of the ramparts, leaving the centre of the site open.

These excavations changed the picture of Iron Age Herefordshire quite dramatically. The Celtic folk who left France in search of new land may have built impressively fortified settlements, but they did not introduce the hillfort idea into this part of the world. Thriving hilltop centres existed centuries before. Indeed, thanks to radiocarbon dating, we now know the tradition goes back at least to 900 BC, a time before iron-working was known in Europe. Excavations at the Breiddin, a hillfort in Powys, have recovered evidence of an ancient eighth century BC bronze-using comunity who lived in a walled hilltop settlement overlooking the River Severn. This consisted of a cluster of possibly rectangular huts set within an enclosure which was subsequently destroyed by fire. In the past, it has been fashionable in archaeology to explain new features in the archaeological record as the result of invasion or migration. No doubt such folk movements did occur in prehistory, bringing change in their wake. Perhaps the Celts did enter Britain between 400 and 250 BC. Perhaps Croft Ambrey was the work of another foreign element, possessing a different cultural tradition—this has certainly been suggested. However, to view change in this way is to play down the continuity of our native culture. Most hillforts are an Iron Age phenomenon. However, their origins can be traced back further, to climatic and social changes that were beginning in Europe sometime after about 1200 BC.

Capler Camp

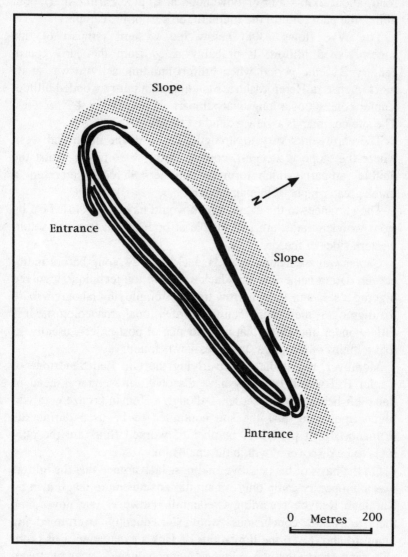

Slope

Slope

Entrance

Entrance

N

0   Metres   200

A smaller hillfort with wide views over the countryside
Location: 2.5km south of Fownhope (SO 593 329)
Access: Via a public footpath which runs along the ramparts

A public footpath leads up from the B4224, Hereford to Ross road, about 2km south of Fownhope at Caplor Farm. After about 400m, the path follows the southern rampart of the camp.

The Wye flows 130m below the western rampart of this superbly-sited hillfort. It probably dates from the early fourth century BC, the period when hillfort-building activity was at its most intense in Herefordshire. Standing on a partly wooded hilltop, Capler consists of a long oval rampart encompassing 4.1 hectares. The site commands a view extending to 45km.

The earthworks vary in strength. Those to the north and west, where the slope is steepest, consist simply of ditches, whilst the double ramparts which form the southern defences represent a much greater input of human labour.

The entrances to the camp, which would have been closed off by stout wooden gates, are still visible at both the eastern and south-western sides of the site.

Capler was excavated by G.H. Jack in 1924, long before radio-carbon dating came into use. Jack's excavation technique involved digging a series of long, narrow trenches employing labourers to do the digging as there were then few professional archaeologists. It is little wonder, therefore, that no evidence of post-holes—usually all that remains of Iron Age structures—was found.

Moreover, the acidic soil overlying the Old Red Sandstone of Capler Hill would probably have dissolved any pottery, metal or bone left behind by the settlers—though a Roman bronze coin was found, indicating that the site continued to be used during the Romano-British period. A number of worked flints are the only tools to be discovered within the enclosure.

On the basis of his negative findings, Jack argued that the hillfort was a temporary camp only—a similar conclusion to that drawn by Kathleen Kenyon regarding Credenhill. However, we now know that Kenyon's conclusions were subsequently overturned by Stanford and, given the limitations of Jack's excavation, it is probably safer to say that the evidence is inconclusive—a small stream at the southern end of the hillfort would certainly have made permanent occupation of the site possible.

Credenhill Camp

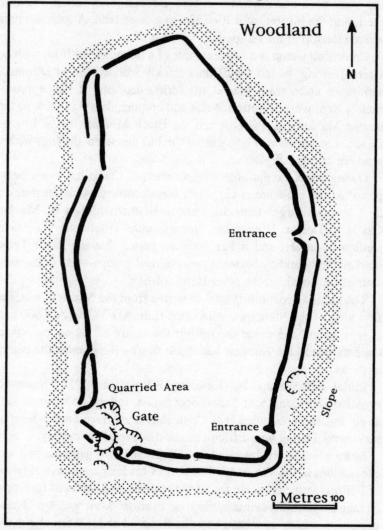

Woodland

N

Entrance

Quarried Area

Gate

Entrance

Slope

0 Metres 100

A large afforested hillfort
Location: Above the village of Credenhill, just to the west of
Hereford (SO 450 446)
Access: By a public footpath, though most of the hillfort lies on
private land

A public footpath runs for about 250m from Credenhill Church to the outer bank and ditch. From here, a rough track spirals round to the top of the hillfort, which stands on private land. A footpath runs around the top of the rampart.

Credenhill Camp is a fine example of a univallate hillfort, with an internal spring, which stands on a thickly wooded hill of Dittonian sandstone underneath glacial till (drift) deposits. It lies approximately 8km west of Sutton Walls and commands a fine view to the distant Malverns to the east and the Black Mountains and Brecon Beacons to the west. The sides of the hill are steep-sloping, with a gradient of 1 in 3 in places.

Owing to its exceptional size, Credenhill Camp has been interpreted as the pre-Roman capital of Herefordshire. At 20 hectares it is 2 hectares larger than the famous southern hillfort of Maiden Castle in Dorset. Within the vicinity, only Titterstone Clee near Ludlow is larger, and it has been suggested that the River Teme marked the boundary between two political groups—one occupying southern Shropshire, the other Herefordshire.

The name Credenhill is said to derive from the Saxon Creda, the first king of the Mercians, who ruled from AD 583 to AD 600 and is reputed to have made the hillfort the centre of his operations in the area just as the Romans had made nearby Kenchester the centre of theirs.

Initial excavations by Kathleen Kenyon in 1951, however, revealed no evidence of Saxon occupation, indeed no trace of huts at all and she concluded that Credenhill must have been a temporary camp. Dating was difficult as she discovered no pottery.

More clues were revealed by Dr S. Stanford who carried out excavations at the site in 1963 as part of his long term investigation of hillforts in the area. He found the remains of a series of four-post rectangular structures measuring on average 3.6m x 2.4m. These structures, which may have had floors raised about 0.5m above the ground, were timber-framed, single-storey buildings probably with wattle-and-daub infilling and ridge roofs.

Although the excavated area of any hillfort—and especially one as large as Credenhill—is of necessity small in relation to the total area of the site, Stanford suggested that these buildings may originally have covered the whole of the interior, set in lines forming a regular gridiron layout similar to the sections of the interiors he had excavated at Croft Ambrey, Herefordshire Beacon and Midsummer Hill.

If the structures were indeed houses rather than granaries, they would have been rather cramped, but even so Stanford estimated that they could have accommodated families of four or five. On the basis of this calculation he was able to suggest that Credenhill Camp, during its most populous phase, could have supported a population of 3,600-4,800—greater than that of most Herefordshire settlements today.

Other features of the site gave Stanford a clue as to the date of the settlement. He suggested, on the basis of firmer evidence obtained from radiocarbon dating, that around 390 BC a series of innovations appeared in hillfort design. One of these was the 'guard-room'. Another was the complex 'inturned entrance'. The inturned entrances at Credenhill can be traced at the east and south-east of the site.

He argued that these innovations were introduced by immigrants from the continent, the same Iron Age B people whom Kathleen Kenyon first identified at Sutton Walls and who brought elements of early La Téne culture to these shores. Their characteristic 'duck-stamped' pottery was not found although some pottery fragments did come to light. These contained grits which suggest that at least some of the pottery on this site, as on other hillfort sites within the county, was manufactured in the Malvern area during the Iron Age.

Stanford, however, argued that the Iron Age B people arrived in the area far earlier than Kenyon imagined and that they penetrated farther north, founding new settlements such as Credenhill and Sutton Walls, and enlarging Herefordshire Beacon, Wall Hills, Little Doward Camp and Croft Ambrey among others. In addition to introducing guard rooms and inturned entrances, these people also initiated the system of excavating the material for their ramparts from quarries located inside the defences.

Croft Ambrey

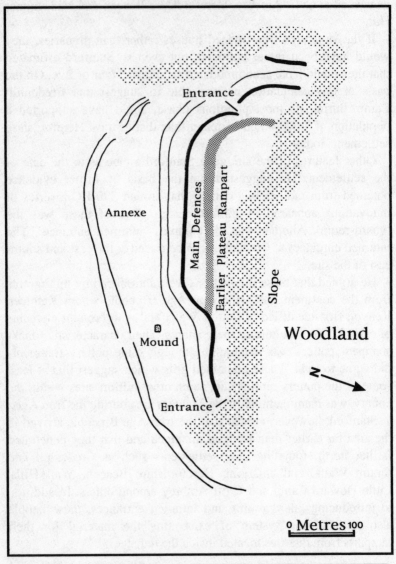

Entrance

Annexe

Main Defences

Earlier Plateau Rampart

Slope

Mound

Woodland

N

Entrance

0 Metres 100

Hillfort sited above a steep-sided scarp
Location: 3km north of Croft Castle, near Yarpole (SO 445 688)
Access: Via a public footpath which leads from Croft Castle

Croft Ambrey is a National Trust property accessible at all times through the grounds of Croft Castle. Croft Castle is signposted off the B4362 Ludlow to Presteigne road between the villages of Lucton and Bircher. A footpath leads from the car park at Croft Castle to the hillfort about 2km away.

It is said, with little or no evidence, that the fifteenth century Welsh rebel Owain Glyndwr once occupied this, one of the most famous and majestic hillforts in the Marches.

Fifteen hundred years earlier, another Celtic resistance leader, Caratacos, is believed to have fallen back on Croft Ambrey during his protracted struggle with the Roman governor Ostorius Scapula.

For archaeologists, however, Croft Ambrey is a landmark in the recent history of the discipline. During the 1960s, Dr Stanley Stanford led an excavation which, over the course of six seasons, provided a completely revised set of Iron Age dates for the Marches. Previously, archaeologists had relied upon dates worked out in 1931 by Professor Christopher Hawkes. Stanford, however, was able to demonstrate that Hawkes's dates were much too recent. He showed that the earliest timber enclosures, which preceded the earthen ramparts at some Marches hillfort sites and which had been dated to around 450 BC, were at least a century older.

Stanford arrived at his early dates by concentrating upon the gateways at Croft Ambrey. By careful excavation, he worked out that these had been rebuilt twenty times during the lifetime of the fort and that each new set of posts had lasted roughly thirty years. Stanford was then able to pin-point the absolute dates of the gate timbers using the new technique of radiocarbon dating and to tie this information in with the rebuilding phases he had discovered in the ground.

Stanford therefore stated confidently that prehistoric building work began at Croft Ambrey around 550 BC. At this time hillfort builders on the southern chalklands were busy constructing the first defences at the massive site of Danebury in Wessex. Unlike Danebury, however, which yielded evidence of round houses, the structures at Croft Ambrey were rectangular.

The choice of position was excellent—a long, narrow hill of Silurian limestone with a very steep scarp to the north which needed no artificial defence.

Iron sword found at Croft Ambrey

Here, the Iron Age settlers set to work constructing a simple ditch and rampart enclosing a relatively small area of 2.2 hectares. This forms the so-called 'plateau camp', which stands some 305m above sea level.

Stanford argued that the first defences were the work of invaders. Whoever they were, these newcomers seem to have lacked pottery-making skills as no pottery fragments at all were discovered in these early levels. It is probable that they used perishable materials such as wood and leather for the everyday domestic purposes of preparing food and carrying water.

These mysterious people also heralded a revolution in house building and early town planning. The Iron Age norm of haphaz-ardly-arranged roundhouses was rejected at Croft Ambrey in favour of regularly-spaced four-post houses laid out barrack-like along the streets.

This layout was retained right up until the Roman invasion. During this long period of occupation, individual dwellings were rebuilt up to six times in exactly the same spot. Clearly, people felt that if a house was good enough for their parents and grandparents, it was, with the necessary repairs, good enough for them.

Only speculation about the social rules which lay behind this strict adherence to an established living pattern is possible. The village may not simply have been a cluster of houses occupied by individual households. It may have been subdivided into larger units such as neighbourhoods, perhaps representing different segments of the same clan. These blocks may have been rigidly demarcated and maintained over many generations, forcing people to use the same house plot again and again. It is well-known how territorially-minded neighbours can be—especially if their right to a plot of land has been in the family for some time. The lines of demarcation need not necessarily leave evidence for an archaeologist to discover, they may only have been imaginary lines inscribed on the mental map of individual villagers.

Not all of the buildings discovered were dwellings. Like all Iron Age communities, the Croft Ambrey people needed to store food, particularly wheat. Adequate supplies were needed for bread and porridge throughout the year and for next year's sowing. The excavators noted that in many of the structures, which were otherwise indistinguishable from houses, burnt or 'carbonised' wheat grains had survived to the present day. They labelled these structures granaries, and the large number found in the settlement reinforces the idea that the hillforts functioned in part as secure food stores.

The staple diet of bread and porridge was supplemented by meat, though domesticated animals served more than one purpose. Stanford has suggested that the large number of pig bones may reflect the fact that there was more forest available in this area for pannage: or that the pigs were used as substitute 'ploughs' to break up new ground. Few young sheep bones were discovered, suggesting that these may have been bred for wool rather than being slaughtered for meat, though mutton as opposed to lamb was the favoured meat of even recent generations.

The next surge of activity at Croft Ambrey came around 390 BC, when a massive new rampart was constructed. The great wall, which measured 28m in width and twelve in height, was built outside the old circuit. This wall, which still stands to a height of seven metres, increased the total enclosed area to 5.8 hectares. Then, about sixty years later, another innovation appeared: the north-western entrance, which had consisted of a seven metre wide passage-way leading to a double gate, was redesigned. The passage shrank to four metres but was lengthened, and the original double portal was replaced by a single one. Forcing any invader into a longer, narrower passage-way would presumably make it easier for the defenders to pick them off with sling-stones, which have been found in great numbers on many hillforts throughout Britain. Also at this time, the first stone and timber guard rooms appeared in Herefordshire, Shropshire and Cheshire. Two were built at the entrance to Croft Ambrey, using sandstone from the base of the hill; and they have been found also at Midsummer Hill, Malvern. Timber guard-rooms are known earlier at Midsummer Hill and also possibly at Credenhill. These are parallelled by structures found at Maiden Castle in Wessex. It is not until around 330 BC, however, that they are found with stone footings. About 80 BC wooden walk-ways for patrolling sentries were erected over the gateway, by which time the system of guard rooms had long been abandoned.

Stanford argues that the occupation of Croft Ambrey ended sometime around the middle of the first century AD when the Romans gained control of the area. Rather than being a Silurian stronghold, he believes it was occupied by the Deceangli, who were forced out by Scapula's advance.

To the south of the early plateau camp and the later main camp there is a relatively weak 'annexe' of 4.8 hectares which was found to contain a very interesting ritual site obscured by bracken, and soon to be known as The Mound.

In the Autumn of 1965, Stanford's team began an investigation of The Mound, which led to the discovery of a nearby terrace and several scoops. Excavation began in earnest the following Easter. As the work progressed, some of the most convincing evidence that we have found for Late Iron Age ritual in Herefordshire began to emerge.

It seems that about a generation after the destruction of the main village at Croft Ambrey in AD 48 or thereabouts, Iron Age people returned to the abandoned settlement, not to live but to carry out periodic religious ceremonies.

Around AD 75, when the Romans had gained control of the Marches, these people constructed a raised ceremonial floor, about 8.5 x 6.7m, which they sprinkled with red clay, symbolising, in Dr Stanford's opinion, blood or the sun.

Into this floor were dug several fire-pits, one of which contained a pig skull. Smaller holes contained charcoal and at the south of the platform was the most compelling find of all—a deposit of clay objects, each resembling the ox-head motif commonly found in Celtic art. These may have been tokens placed in the ground as a foundation deposit when the platform was built.

Also found on or near the floor were numerous bone fragments of sheep, goats and cattle, suggesting that animal sacrifices were habitually offered up by the priests. The large quantity of broken pottery, coupled with evidence from elsewhere, may indicate that the sacrificial animals were subsequently eaten by those taking part in the ritual.

Somewhat later, and perhaps following another period of abandonment, a large squarish flat-topped mound was built over the platform. This raised the ceremonial area to 1.5m above the general level. The mound was about 11.6m square and resembled the plan of Romano-Celtic temples at Colchester and Woodeaton. Around three sides, and still standing to a height of 0.38m in places, were several courses of limestone kerbing. With the change in form came a change in the nature of the ceremonies held at Croft Ambrey. Whatever the new rituals were, they appear to have involved less fire-making and pot-breaking than the earlier version.

For 100 years this remained the scene of ceremonial activity, perhaps led by druids before their cult was finally extinguished. The only other convincing evidence of Late Iron Age ritual in the county comes from Peterchurch in the Golden Valley. This too is in the form of a mound, sited near the hillfort of Poston and excavated by George Marshall in 1933. Marshall found no burials inside the barrow, but he did discover several hearths similar to those Stanford found on the ceremonial floor at Croft Ambrey. An irregular mound at Midsummer Hill may offer another parallel in the county, though this is highly dubious.

It is important to emphasise that these ceremonial sites appear very late in the Iron Age archaeological record, dating from a time when the Roman presence in the area was becoming established. Apart, possibly, from Wapley, the date of which is uncertain, no earlier Celtic ritual sites are known in the county, which is hardly surprising when we learn from the classical sources that Celtic sacred places were located in out of the way forest groves. If these consisted of simple structures like the original open-air ceremonial floor at Croft Ambrey, it is unlikely that any further evidence will come to light.

Dinedor Camp

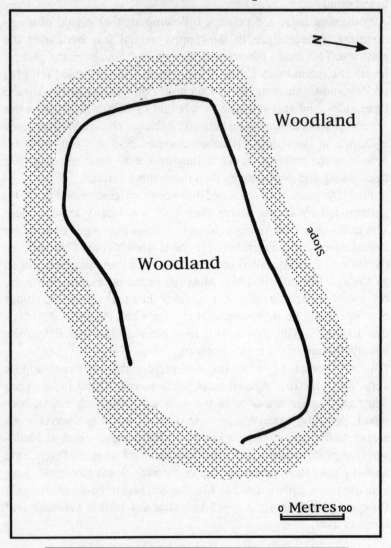

Woodland

Woodland

Slope

N

0 Metres 100

A medium-sized hillfort
Location: 4km south of Hereford (S0 510 363)
Access: The whole site is open to the public
with wooden steps giving access over the rampart

From Hereford take the A49 Ross road, and turn left on the B4399 Holme Lacy road about 1km south of the River Wye. Take the first right-hand turn signposted Dinedor. Bear left after 2.5km and then sharp left after 0.5km. This road skirts the western side of Dinedor Hill and after about 1km a steep road on the right leads up to a parking area adjoining the ramparts.

Formerly called Oyster Hill Camp, the univallate hillfort covers an area of 3.5 hectares and was bequeathed to the city of Hereford in the 1980s. It commands a very good defensive position over-looking the Wye Valley, just as Sutton Walls overlooks the Lugg. The name 'Dinedor' is Celtic, meaning 'fortified hill' and refers to the 8m high rampart which today only stands at the north-east of the site. Originally it may have enclosed the entire settlement, with a main entrance at the east.

Dinedor Camp was probably built by the same group of Iron Age B immigrants, identified by their distinctive 'duck-stamped' pottery, who settled at Sutton Walls. This is the conclusion of Kathleen Kenyon, who excavated both sites, though her work at Dinedor was very limited.

These Continental people, she believed, originally penetrated northwards after landing on the coast of Cornwall sometime after 260 BC. They followed the coast and river valleys as far as Herefordshire where they settled, developing a network of prosperous farming communities which survived for many centuries. During its most populous phase, from the first century BC, through the period of the Roman conquest to the second century AD, as many as 1,200 people may have lived at Dinedor.

It is now believed that Sutton Walls, Credenhill and other sites date from around 390 BC, and though immigrants may have entered Herefordshire at about this time, they did not introduce the hillfort idea. Croft Ambrey dates from around 550 BC and the Breiddin, just over the border in Powys, is even earlier. It seems the hillfort idea evolved in the area as a result of indigenous social processes originating in the Bronze Age. Moreover, Kathleen Kenyon suggests that the immigrants developed a network of farming communities, suggesting an unlikely degree of peaceful co-existence between hillfort communities. The hillforts probably represent autonomous and economically self-sufficient clans which were only welded together into a larger political entity under Caratacos at the time of the Roman invasion.

This does not devalue the work carried out by Kathleen Kenyon in the late nineteen-forties and early fifties. Her evidence continues to be useful in helping to reconstruct the economic life of hillfort communities, who may have overseen the agricultural producers living in smaller settlements scattered throughout their territory.

The excavations at Dinedor Camp revealed a community whose diet consisted of cereals, notably wheat and barley, and meat. Sickles for harvesting the grain were found on the site, as were quern stones used to produce flour for making bread and porridge. Cattle were a very important form of wealth in Iron Age society, valued for their milk and for their strength, as well as for their meat. Similarly, sheep and goats, which seem to have been of secondary importance to cattle, were kept to provide wool and milk.

The wool was probably plucked or combed from the sheep when they were moulting and then spun to form yarn which could be coloured using vegetable dyes and woven on upright looms. It seems the finished product was in great demand overseas. Woollen cloaks made by the ancient Britons were a much sought after fashion accessory in Rome! Loom weights, which held the warp threads during the weaving process, and also a weaving comb were found on the site.

Much of the information on diet came from the daily rubbish these people left behind them. Many generations lived at Dinedor and their domestic activities caused the build-up of thick occupation levels containing many animal bones and dense charcoal deposits. It seems the preferred living area was at the rear of the ramparts. This arrangement of living space contrasts with the pattern found on sites such as Credenhill, Herefordshire Beacon and Croft Ambrey where structures (huts and granaries) seem to have covered virtually the whole of the interior, whilst Kenyon's suggested parent site at Sutton Walls has been too badly damaged by recent quarrying to give any useful comparison. Perhaps the open centre at Dinedor was used for threshing grain or for corralling cattle.

Pottery was found within the remains of Iron Age huts, which also produced part of an iron axe-head and a few bone tools.

Herefordshire Beacon or British Camp

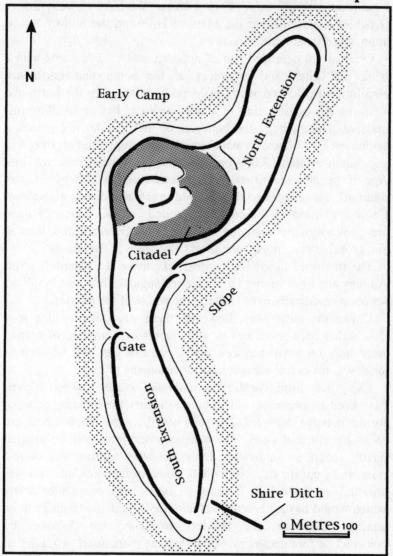

Hillfort with massive ramparts and panoramic views
Location: On top of the Malverns, just off the A449 (SO 760 400)
Access: Via a public path from a car park

Herefordshire Beacon is easily approached via a footpath leading from a car park off the A449 as it crosses the hills. However, there is public access all over the Malvern Hills and the hillfort can be approached from many directions.

Originally a defended site of approximately 3.2 hectares with a bank and ditch and entrances at the south and north-east, Herefordshire Beacon was considerably enlarged to the north and south by the construction of a later defence. For about 2km, this massive rampart hugs the contours of the hillside. It encloses a settlement of 13 hectares which might have supported an Iron Age population of some 2,000 people. These may have been the Iron Age B people, identified by Kathleen Kenyon and by Stanley Stanford, who suggested they arrived in the area during a period of Celtic expansion on the continent around 390 BC. Certainly there are similarities between the settlement on Herefordshire Beacon and probable contemporary hillforts elsewhere in the county.

The structures inside the rampart, like those at Credenhill, Croft Ambrey and Midsummer Hill, were rectangular, four-post buildings set out methodically over virtually the whole of the interior.

Unlike the other sites, however, these structures—which may have either been dwellings or grain stores or a mixture of both—were built on small terraces. These terraces can still be seen in shadow form as the sun is setting, covering the hilltop.

Using only primitive digging tools and wicker baskets, it must have been an immense undertaking to quarry the building material for the massive defences. The soils overlying the igneous Malvern rocks are thin and stony. The material came from both an internal quarry scoop, an innovation found on other hillfort sites at this time, and from the defensive ditch. Some of the ditch material was also thrown down hill, forming an outer bank or counter scarp, which would have presented yet another formidable obstacle to an attacker. However, the builders weakened the defences by constructing four entrances, rather than the more usual two. Each of these would have been vulnerable to attack from battering and fire.

It seems reasonable to assume that the community was led by one or more powerful people who were able to mobilise a large workforce, but there is little evidence of social differentiation within the settlement.

It has been suggested that hillforts such as Herefordshire Beacon were principally central places within a clan territory where the harvest could be brought and securely stored prior to redistribution among the members of the community. Many of these people may have lived in smaller farming villages on lower ground.

Against the idea that hillforts were permanently occupied settlements is the perennial argument that many lack a water supply, an argument which holds good for the Herefordshire Beacon. One answer is that the villagers may have collected rainwater from the roofs of their huts and stored it in wooden containers. However, if the village was permanently occupied it is more likely that they would have had to descend the hill daily to obtain drinking water from springs to the south and east. The zig-zag path which they may have taken still leads down the hillside from the south gate. Without an internal water supply, however, the defenders of Herefordshire Beacon would have been vulnerable to the kind of siege tactics which were favoured by Roman commanders, but not appreciated at the time of construction.

Early maps indicate two features which are probably of a later date than the hillfort itself and which are still visible today: the so-called 'Citadel' on the summit, and the Shire Ditch or 'Red Earls Dyke'. The former is an earthwork of early Norman date, as pottery of that period was found within the oval shaped bank and ditch, and was a minor timber castle.

The Shire Ditch is a low bank and ditch which runs from the hillfort and links it to nearby Midsummer Hill. It is believed to have been constructed by Gilbert de Clare, Earl of Gloucester about 1287, as a boundary to separate lands belonging to the Bishop of Hereford from those in Malvern Chase.

Ivington Camp

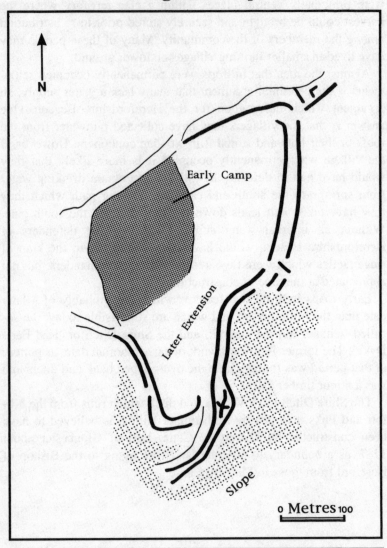

N

Early Camp

Later Extension

Slope

0 Metres 100

A large hillfort now set within woodland
Location: At Brierley, 3km south of Leominster (SO 485 546)
Access: Via a public footpath, though permission is required to
explore the hillfort from Camp Farm, situated within the fort

From the village of Brierley, head west on the minor road and park when you reach the crossroads. Walk for 1km from the crossroads along the bridle track which leads south, towards the western end of the hill. Turn left on to a concrete track, signposted to Camp Farm. The bridleway passes through the fort, but permission to explore the enclosure can be obtained from Camp Farm, situated within the hillfort.

It has an inturned entrance at the south-east, typical of the hillfort phase which commenced around 390 BC, perhaps the work of incoming Celtic La Téne groups from Northern France.

Some of Ivington's former grandeur has been ploughed and quarried away over the years; but a substantial inner rampart—complete with walkway—still stands 6m above the triangular enclosure.

The fort consists of double ramparts and ditch and is well protected to the north-west, west and south-east by precipitous natural slopes of old red sandstone. The 9 hectare site would have offered superb natural protection to the inhabitants and their food supplies. The position would also have made Ivington Camp a highly visible territorial marker within the landscape.

The farm track to the east is modern. The entrance at the north-east, however, is original and was protected by earthworks which have since been ploughed out. The more complex inturned entrance to the south-east is approached by a hollow way. This is flanked on the right side by two ramparts. It has been suggested that the massive cruciform earthwork between these ramparts supported some kind of watch-tower.

The smaller 3.1 hectare enclosure in the north-western corner of the camp was probably the original settlement, its crescent-shaped earthwork, like the earliest defences at Sutton Walls and Croft Ambrey pre-dating the Celtic migrations of 390 BC.

When these people arrived in Herefordshire, the hillfort was considerably enlarged to the east and the inturned entrance constructed. Contemporary building work took place on a similar scale at Herefordshire Beacon and Wall Hills, Ledbury.

Although Ivington has not received the intensive archaeological investigation of Croft Ambrey, Sutton Walls and others, similar evidence of a predominantly self-sufficient farming economy could be expected.

Thus, we might expect to find cattle, sheep and pig bones and the occasional bones of wild animals such as deer, hunted for their antlers as well for food. Also sickles, pottery and loom weights. Perhaps one or two prestige items might turn up—metal swords or La Téne brooches.

Judging by the size of the site, which is one of Herefordshire's larger hillforts (see Appendix 1), Ivington Camp may have supported a population of around 1,400 people. The authors, however, have seen no estimation of the number of huts the enclosure may have originally contained.

Midsummer Hill

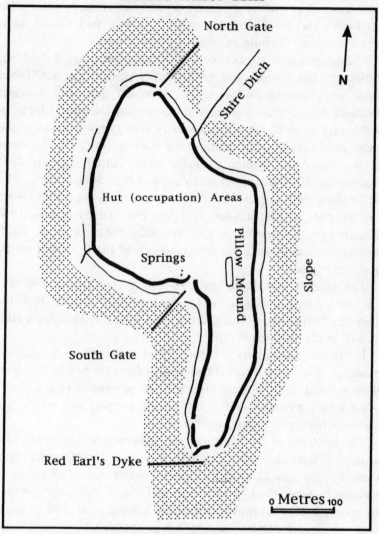

North Gate

Shire Ditch

Hut (occupation) Areas

Springs

Pillow Mound

Slope

South Gate

Red Earl's Dyke

N

0 Metres 100

Description: A large hillfort
Location: On top of the Malverns,
south of British Camp (SO 760 375)
Access: Via footpath from British Camp,
or from a car park off the A438 to its south

The hillfort can be reached either by a footpath leading off the car park on the A449 where it crosses the Malvern Hills, in which case head south and past British Camp; or from a car park on the A438 where it crosses the hills, in which case head north.

Midsummer Hill was the scene of much archaeological dabbling during the last century and in the earlier part of this one. Often these early excavations were not recorded and their remains confused later archaeologists, who sometimes interpreted them as prehistoric features. Only occasionally was mention made in the archives of such amateur archaeological work—in the Transactions of the Woolhope Naturalists Field Club, Alfred Watkins does mention the 1924 investigations by the Rev H.L. Somers-Cox.

Between 1965 and 1970 the first truly scientific excavations were carried out at Midsummer Hill by Dr Stanley Stanford of Birmingham University, whose previous excavations at Croft Ambrey produced valuable new evidence of the Iron Age of the Marches region.

The rampart and ditch, probably constructed around 390 BC, enclose an area of 8.6 hectares. The perimeter takes in both the summit of Midsummer Hill and the ridge of nearby Hollybush Hill, as well as the intervening dip.

In places—particularly at the north end and south gates—there is evidence of a counterscarp, or secondary bank formed by the spoil thrown downhill from the ditch. Inside the rampart there is a quarry ditch which provided spoil for the main rampart and which is a common feature of hillforts of this period.

The hardness of the Malvern rock, however, would have made quarrying difficult, especially with primitive digging equipment. Consequently, the rampart-builders of Midsummer Hill chose to construct a relatively low earth wall and to give this a vertical face by adding a stone revetment. Again, the igneous rock, with its irregular jointing, presented a problem. It is quite unsuitable for use as dry stone walling and the builders had to look elsewhere for the material they needed. They found it about a mile away, where an outcrop of Llandovery sandstone provided an excellent source of sedimentary rock suitable for their needs.

The job of quarrying the sandstone and transporting it to the site would have involved a considerable level of organisation. Did they bring the stone to the site in carts? If so they would have had to build roads. The truth is we do not know how the task was carried out, nor how many people were involved. Stanford remarks, however, that the defences were probably erected quickly, 'assuming they were vital for survival, and not simply a matter of prestige.'

There seem to be two original entrances to the settlement, marked by an inturning of the ramparts—another typical feature of hillforts of this period. Other breaks in the defences are probably more recent, as they show no signs of inturning. A map of 1870 drawn by H.H. Lines records a 'chariot road' approaching the north gate. However, Stanford found no rutting in the road to confirm that it had been used by wheeled transport; and neither here nor at Croft Ambrey, where a similar roadway was found, did any chariot fittings come to light.

Pottery found during the 1924 investigations was duck-stamped and similar to sherds discovered at Bredon Hill in Worcestershire. Unlike that hillfort, however, there was no evidence at all inside the defences for the stone foundations of circular huts, generally considered by earlier archaeologists to be the Iron Age norm. At Midsummer Hill, all the structures discovered were of wood and fell into two types: those based upon an oblong arrangement of posts, and those, also oblong, based on cill beams (the usual later 'black and white' cottage style)—the former type predominating.

In common with neighbouring Herefordshire Beacon, Stanford found numerous semi-circular platforms between three and nine metres in diameter. It was upon these platforms, which seem to have been used again and again, that the oblong structures were built. A little daub found by the excavators sugests that a wattle and daub technique was used in the construction of the huts, about half of which contained hearths and were therefore interpreted as dwellings. No trace of roofing material was found, indicating that roofs were probably made of perishable materials such as thatch or skins.

The structures—whether dwellings or other buildings such as granaries—were apparently laid out about 4.5m apart and conformed as closely to a regular gridiron pattern as topography would allow. Judging by the estimated number of huts, the population of Midsummer Hill may have been as high as 1,300 to 1,500 people, some of whom were keen on personal adornment, as shown by the discovery of shale, pottery and glass beads. The existence of an internal spring behind the southern gate meant there was a continuous supply of fresh water available to the population. This offers a plausible argument for permanent occupation of the site.

We can only guess that these people's economy was based on farming, as the acidic Malvern soils would have destroyed any animal bones left behind by the inhabitants. Unusually, however, no querns (used for grinding grain) were found on the site, though many sherds of a crude earthenware material known as VCP suggests the existence of ovens for baking bread. Stanford imagines a varied agricultural hinterland surrounding the hillfort, extending for about a mile in all directions and consisting of ploughland, grazing and forest pannage.

Following on from the duck stamped pottery, a new type with a different kind of decoration appears in the archaeological evidence for Midsummer Hill. This decoration consists of diagonal lines, chevrons and lattice patterns. It has been argued that this pottery indicates the arrival of newcomers or new influences in the area shortly before the Roman invasion.

In general, however, Stanford believes the total finds, though few, 'are sufficient to allow us to see that the occupants of Midsummer Hill shared in a general way the traditions of western Iron Age Britain in tools, ornament and economy.'

Certainly, they seem to have shared with their contemporaries a way of disposing of their dead which left no trace in the hillfort. In common with all other hillforts on the Welsh border, there is no sign of burial, cremation or any other recognized means of getting rid of the deceased. Neither is there any sign of coinage—which does appear on more southerly hillforts towards the end of the Iron Age—although two hoards of currency bars were discovered near Great Malvern in 1856 and 1857.

The south gate at Midsummer Hill was chosen by Stanford for intensive investigation, following the success of the Croft Ambrey gateway excavation which revealed a dateable sequence of repairs. During five season's work at Midsummer Hill, 17 successive sets of gateposts were identified spanning a period of 450 years. The style of entrance architecture was generally similar to that at Croft Ambrey, as was the overall gateway plan, with its deeply inturned entrance forming a 6.2 metre wide corridor with a timber guard room on either side. The gateway complex has been compared with that of Maiden Castle in Dorset and Stanford suggests this supports the idea that 'new chieftains' entered Britain from northern France at this time, bringing their design of duck-stamped pottery with them. Stanford further suggests that this arrival was broadly contemporary with historically dated folk movements on the continent which occurred when Celtic peoples moved out of their Danubian homeland early in the fourth century BC.

These Iron Age B people are generally seen as the founders of many hillforts in Herefordshire. These include Midsummer Hill, though Stanford does not rule out the possibility of an earlier settlement on the summit of the hill. The main settlement lasted for 450 years until the Roman conquest in AD 48 when, in common with many other hillforts, it seems the occupation of Midsummer ended violently—many of the huts show signs of destruction by fire.

Later, in the Medieval period, it appears the site was ploughed for agricultural use—though yields from the meagre soils must have been low. Another indication of Medieval use is the pillow mound at the east of the site. This has been interpreted as a rabbit warren, consisting of loose soil in which rabbits could breed and be easily caught. However, an irregular low oval mound about nine metres in diameter to the north of the pillow mound is less certainly assigned to the Medieval period. Stanford has seen a possible parallel between this feature and the ritual mound in the annexe at Croft Ambrey.

Poston Camp

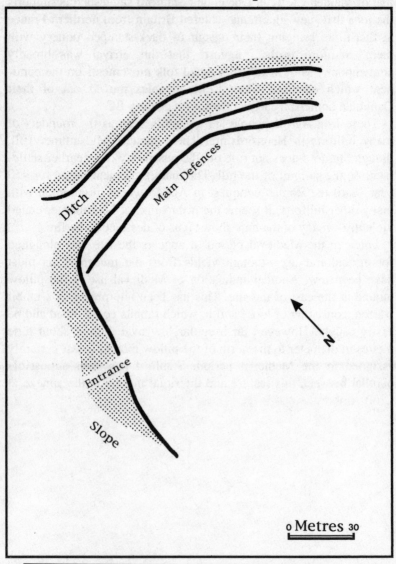

Ditch

Main Defences

Entrance

Slope

N

0 Metres 30

A small camp, possibly settled by Bronze Age people
Location: Just south of Vowchurch (SO 359 377)
Access: A public path passes within 200m of its eastern side

Poston Camp stands on private land, but a public footpath from the B4348 Kingstone to Peterchurch road passes within 200m of the eastern side of the hillfort. The hillfort is 75m from the main road.

'Flints found in the area indicate that the site was frequented by man from an early period'. So begins Dr I.E. Anthony's report on his excavation at Poston in 1958. The flints, which were also found in scatters in nearby fields, were regarded as evidence that either Bronze Age or Neolithic groups had occupied this area before the Iron Age and long before the Romano-British settlers who were identified during earlier work at the site between 1932 and 1937.

It was not until the arrival of Celtic culture by invasion or by the transmission of ideas, however, that any form of defensive work was carried out at the site. Owing to the similarities of the objects discovered at Poston with those from other Herefordshire hillforts, Dr Anthony suggested that these Celts were the same Iron Age B people of French origin identified at Bredon Hill (Worcestershire), Pen Dinas (Dyfed), Sutton Walls, Aconbury and elsewhere. He states they were 'probably stock breeders who wandered up through the Welsh Marches in search of fresh pastures'.

Following Kathleen Kenyon, Dr Anthony argued that they arrived in the area around 100 BC, bringing their characteristic 'duck-stamped' pottery with them. The results from radiocarbon dating, however, suggest their arrival was likely to have been between 390 and 250 BC.

An alternative interpretation of the site was offered by George Marshall, who undertook the original excavation in the 1930's. He grouped Poston together with nearby Timberline Camp and Walterstone Camp and suggested that they should be viewed as distinct from the larger Wye/Lugg group. All three hillforts lie in the Monnow Basin and Marshall argued that they are a relatively late imitation of the Wye/Lugg forts by a Bronze Age population inhabiting the hills in the west of Herefordshire.

It may seem odd to suggest that the hillfort could be the work of Bronze Age people so late in the Iron Age; however, the discovery of a dozen or so bronze objects from the Roman levels at Poston indicate that there really were no clear breaks between the Bronze Age, the Iron Age and the Roman period. Old traditions continued, although it should be added that during the latter periods bronze was used mainly for decorative items, rather than for tools and weapons as it had been in the past; the bronze pieces found at Poston were all of a special type of brooch known as a fibula.

Whoever they were, it seems the inhabitants of Poston Camp were not cereal growers. No evidence of cereals is cited in the excavation report, at any rate. Proximity to the upland areas of the Black Mountains suggests the inhabitants of Poston practised a pastoral farming economy, making use of grazing on higher pastures, rather than growing cereals in large quantities, although cereal growing cannot be ruled out. However, though bones of the main domesticated animals—cattle, sheep and pigs—were discovered in the Iron Age levels, none occurred in great number. The sheep bones were those of full grown animals, but the sample recovered does not seem to have been large enough to say whether sheep were kept primarily for meat or for wool. Clearly, wool was needed for textile manufacture, as indicated by the presence of seven spindle whorls, made from a variety of materials including bone, lead, earthenware and sandstone. The excavators also found a bone weaving comb.

Human skull fragments were found in three areas of the fort, although these were too small to be of much use to archaeologists. There is some uncertainty about the methods used by Iron Age people to dispose of their dead. In the main text we mentioned the rich Iron Age burials found on Humberside and on the continent. In Europe, there are several major sites consisting of a hillfort and associated burial mounds dating from the earlier Iron Age. One such complex is that of the Heuneberg and Hohmichele on the upper reaches of the Danube in southern Germany. Dr Anthony suggests that a barrow near to the hillfort at Poston is one such Iron Age burial mound, but there is no firm evidence to substantiate this idea. In any case, such mounds would have been reserved for the elite of Celtic society.

Throughout hillforts in Britain, any burials that are found—and given the postulated large populations of these sites there are remarkably few—tend to be in rubbish pits and ditches. If not battle victims, as those at Sutton Walls seem to have been, they may be the remains of 'unclean' members of society, like criminals, disposed of as rubbish! Certainly, peoples such as the Ashanti of West Africa followed a similar practice as recently as the last century. Perhaps the skull fragments at Poston were all that remained of individuals who had transgressed the social norms of their day.

The vast bulk of the population—those not of aristocratic birth and non-criminals—may have been subject to a quite different form of treatment at death which may have been more closely related to a specific sacred area, perhaps near water or in a forest. An interesting possibility is that the dead were not buried at all, but, like the Masai of East Africa, the Parsees and North American Indian tribal peoples, were 'excarnated'—with the corpses laid out on open-air wooden platforms well away from habitation and left to decompose. If this were the case, these societies probably had some notion of purification. Once the bones were stripped of their flesh by wind, rain and sun, they would lose the taint of death and could be brought back from the sacred area into the community. In the Celtic world, the bones may have been placed in ritual shafts, but again, the evidence for large-scale bone deposition is not convincing.

The idea that excarnation was practiced in the Iron Age has been put forward by a number of reputable archaeologists, as has the suggestion that Iron Age people practiced the most intimate disposal of all—cannibalism. We hasten to emphasise that little if anything in the way of hard evidence exists for either practice.

To return to the more objective aspects of the hillfort, Poston is first recorded as a 'camp' on Taylor's county map of 1754, and is known locally as The Rounds. It is a promontory fort situated at the end of a steep-sided spur overlooking the Golden Valley. No internal water supply existed within the comparatively small 1.6 hectare enclosure, but there is a spring outside the defences, a little way down the hillside.

Part of a cobbled road leading through the main gateway on the north-east may have been laid during a late phase of building work, perhaps during the restoration of the defences immediately prior to Frontinus' campaigns in the Marches around AD 70. Also possibly of this later phase is the base of a stone retaining wall against the rampart and a series of post holes for timber lacing. Unlike Sutton Walls, there is no evidence of any destructive episode at Poston, but two late Roman coins of the post-invasion period found on the site indicate its continued use throughout the Roman period.

Sutton Walls

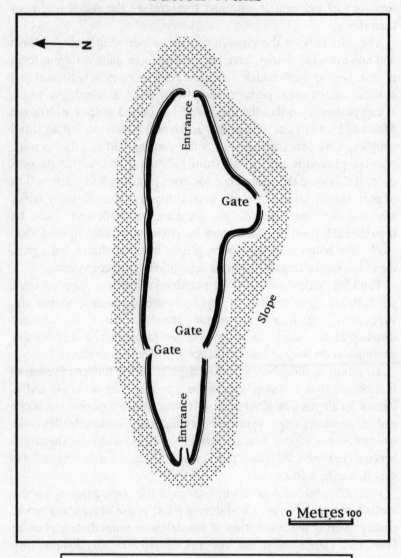

0 Metres 100

A large, but partially damaged, low lying hillfort
Location: About 1km north-west of
Sutton St Nicholas (SO 525 464)
Access: A public path crosses the fort

From Sutton St Nicholas take the road in the direction of Marden. About 1km along this road a track and public footpath leads right to Sutton Walls, from opposite Freens Court Farm.

In the summer of 1948, a team of archaeologists led by Kathleen Kenyon began work at Sutton Walls. The excavation continued for several years, during which time one of the most detailed pictures of Iron Age life in Herefordshire emerged.

Loom weights, weaving combs and spindle whorls; a crucible containing traces of bronze; iron sickles, knives, a dagger, an arrowhead and nails; an anvil; a bronze bracelet and five brooches—these were just some of the items left behind when a thriving Celtic community was forced out of its home by Roman forces.

We might imagine the looms set up in small timber-framed houses, traces of which survived as post holes and fragments of daub. Inside, the houses would have been cramped, poorly-lit and probably smoky, with only a hole in the thatched roof to serve as a chimney.

The sickles would have been used to harvest the grain sown in small fields outside the settlement's walls. But it was not necessarily the inhabitants of the hillfort who farmed, this may have been done by families living in small, lowland hamlets. The evidence from Herefordshire and Worcestershire suggests that lowland settlements ranged in size from villages to single farmsteads.

Once harvested, the corn seems to have been brought into the hillfort where it was threshed on an open floor and winnowed in the wind. Flour was made by grinding the grain between two stones (quern-stones), and seems to have been used for baking small bread rolls, the charred remains of which have been found on other Iron Age sites.

Enormous quantities of sheep, cattle and pig bones discovered at Sutton Walls reveal a community rich in livestock. (The very density of the bone deposits, coupled with the presence of clay, has helped preserve metal, pottery and bone at the site.) But besides keeping domesticated animals and growing cereals, the society also retained elements of its remote ancestors' lifestyle, hunting wild animals such as deer. As well as meat, deer also provided antlers from which tools could be fashioned.

Pottery fragments bearing distinctive 'duck' designs suggest the Celtic people of Sutton Walls were linked to groups using similar designs as far away as Brittany and Portugal. It has been suggested that the Sutton Walls people migrated to the area from Brittany as refugees forced by Germanic raiders to flee their homes around 100 BC. Subsequent advances in dating methods, however, put the date of any possible migration sometime in the early fourth century.

The site they chose to settle covers 12 hectares and stands on a long, low mound of glacial drift deposits, overlooking an important prehistoric routeway leading from the Bristol Channel via the River Wye and along the Teme and Clun valleys to Shropshire, a route which the settlers themselves may have followed.

They were not the first to settle at the site, however, for Iron Age peoples, probably the descendants of a Herefordshire Bronze Age population, first occupied Sutton Walls around the middle of the first millennium BC. This original settlement seems to have been undefended, though it may have been surrounded by a timber palisade. It was not until about 390 BC that a rampart was constructed encircling the summit of the hill and revetted with timber and drystone walling. A ditch cut at the foot of the steep slope provided construction material for the rampart, as did scoops cut into the gravel behind it. Huts were later built in these scoops.

Around AD 25, the ramparts were raised and the huts rebuilt on the same layout. Then, as Roman power extended into the area in the middle of the first century AD, a grisly episode in the history of the settlement occurred. As the Roman army advanced, the ditch at the western entrance was hurriedly recut. Immediately afterwards, many battle-scarred bodies—some of which were decapitated— were thrown into the ditch and covered with a layer of soil. It seems the Romans, under Ostorius Scapula, attacked the settlement, massacred the inhabitants and pulled down the defences over them.

Even so, occupation at Sutton Walls continued, but away from the western end, until around AD 300, when it was turned over to agricultural use.

Excavation has revealed no evidence of Saxon occupation to support the folk-tale that Sutton Walls was the site of one of Offa's palaces. The story of Ethelbert's bloody murder may represent a hazy folk-memory of the actual slaughter which took place there many centuries earlier, though recent work has suggested that Offa may have had a palace at Freens Court, just below the ramparts of Sutton Walls.

Today, however, the site is infamous for being 'one of the biggest disgraces in British archaeology', as stated by James Dyer, an archaeological writer, in 1981. A quarry in ancient times, the site was intensively exploited from 1935, particularly during World War II when gravel was needed for wartime construction. As a result, the western half of the hill was left a shell. This was subsequently infilled with toxic waste, even though the site was at this time a scheduled ancient monument. Consequently there is little remaining for the visitor to see at Sutton Walls, though this should not be allowed to diminish its archaeological importance.

Wapley Hill

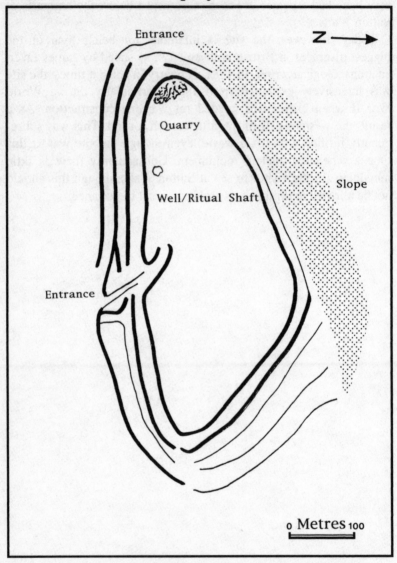

Entrance

Z →

Quarry

Well/Ritual Shaft

Slope

Entrance

0 Metres 100

A wooded hillfort
Location: 3km south-east of Presteigne (SO 345 625)
Access: By new waymarked trail

Wapley Hillfort, to the south of the B4362 Presteigne to Mortimer's Cross road, stands in mixed woodland above the surrounding countryside. Access has recently been improved through a joint venture involving the owners—Forest Enterprise—and Hereford and Worcester County Council. There are now car-parking facilities and a three-mile waymarked trail for visitors.

Perched high on a west-facing escarpment, the hitherto little known camp of Wapley has yielded some of the most compelling evidence for the nature of Celtic religious beliefs and practices in Herefordshire. Indeed, the very form of the earthwork sets it apart from most other hillforts in the county and suggests that it may have had a specialised ritual function during the Iron Age.

The defences, which still stand to a height of about 5.6m, are unusual in their extent, and rivalled only by those at Risbury Camp. On the eastern side, no fewer than five banks were constructed; while four ramparts and ditches were constructed to the south and west, where the natural slope steepens. In all, these defences occupy 6 hectares, while the enclosure itself amounts to just half that area.

In addition, Wapley Hill possesses a magnificent entrance halfway along the southern side of the enclosure. This consists of a 90m passage which turns left towards a concealed gate at the top of the embankment. Another entrance to the north-east is probably of Iron Age date; but the gap at the south-eastern corner is more likely modern.

The most tantalizing feature of all is an apparent sacred well or 'ritual shaft'. The latter, which are often found inside rectilinear earthwork enclosures, have an European ancestry going back well into the Bronze Age. Wilsford Shaft, on Salisbury Plain, may be similar to the Wapley example. Here, a shaft was sunk during the Late Bronze Age into chalk to a depth of 33m. Recovered from the bottom of the shaft was a wooden bowl, bucket fragments (dated between 1470 and 1290 BC), as well as animal bone and other evidence in the form of pollen, molluscs and contemporary soil deposits. Both shafts appear to have been openings to the realm of underworld deities, and as such reflect concepts found in the Greek and Latin worlds. In addition, containing votive deposits of pottery vessels, animal and human bones, and wooden figurines (both male and female in form), such shafts link the cult of the underworld with that of springs and water generally, where Celtic votive deposits are also found.

Sacred wells, on the other hand, seem to appear in the archaeological record much later. Most are of a Romano-Celtic date, with the British examples often associated with Romano-British temples. The wells seem to have been consecrated areas containing holy objects and the sacred remains of ritual activities.

The precise nature of the feature at Wapley remains a mystery; but the discovery within the enclosure of at least four unexcavated pillow mounds increases the likelihood that Wapley was at least in part an Iron Age sacred enclosure. Perhaps the elaborate system of ramparts was an attempt to emphasise symbolically the share of the land apportioned by local Celts to their gods.

Glossary of Terms

Barrow: an artificial mound constructed of chalk debris, earth or turf. Used as a final resting place for one or more people.

Beaker People/Folk: name given to a distinctive pottery tradition and subsequent mortuary practice that is found all over southern and central Britain. The Beaker tradition is also linked to barrows and the first metal work in Britain, ideas often thought to have been brought over by invading peoples from the Continent. However, it is now thought that the Beaker 'invasion' is more a transmission of ideas. In Herefordshire, there is at least one fine example of a Beaker burial located in the Olchon Valley, by the Black Mountains.

Cairn: an artificial mound constructed of stones usually covering one or more burials.

Capstone: a large stone that covers a chambered tomb and is supported by uprights or dry stone walling. Capstones are used on all chambered tombs throughout the Neolithic period. Some capstones possess cupmarks (see below).

Chambered Tomb: earliest form of burial structure, from the Neolithic period, consisting usually of a capstone, a chamber and a series of uprights. Occurs in a number of forms including Portal Dolmens, Passage Graves and Long Mounds. All these three are indigenous to western Britain. During the middle and later Neolithic, tombs became places for many burials. Originally used for single burials, these monuments may also have been used as territorial markers, social, political and ritual meeting places.

Cist: single burial structure, constructed of a series of orthostats (or uprights), synonymous with the Early Bronze Age.

Counterscarp: a bank outside the main hillfort defence produced by throwing spoil from the ditch downhill.

Cupmarks: single and multiple circular gouges cut into rock, usually found on capstones or, in the case of the Golden Valley, on an upright on Arthur's Stone.

Currency Bars: bars of iron believed to have been used as a medium of barter or exchange prior to the introduction of coinage around 100 BC.

Duck-stamped Pottery: Iron Age B hand-made pottery of the West Midlands. The decoration consists of Ss—said to resemble a line of swimming ducks—stamped between two parallel lines.

Halstatt: a site in Austria which gave its name to the first Iron Age culture of Europe, contemporary with British Iron Age A.

Henge: a circular earthen 'doughnut' structure, usually similar in size to a large barrow or stone circle. Late Neolithic or Early Bronze Age in date. It is constructed of a simple circular bank and outlying ditch with entrances to an open central space. Possibly used during ritual or symbolic practices.

Intervisibility: term used to show the mutual visibility between sites, usually with the corresponding style of monument.

La Téne: named after a site in Switzerland, this is the second European Iron Age culture and is broadly contemporary with British Iron Age B.

Megalith: Literally a large stone, from Mega (large) and Lithic (stone).

Microlith: very small flint blade, used for a variety of tasks especially for arrow and spear head inserts. Microliths were used from the Upper Palaeolithic through to the Neolithic.

Multivallate Hillfort: hillfort defences formed by a series of banks and ditches (e.g. Wapley and Risbury).

Pleistocene: geological phase representing the glacial epoch, from 10,000 to 2 million years ago.

Portal Dolmen: burial chamber with porch made from two upright stones supporting a large capstone.

Promontory Hillfort: a hillfort that follows the natural contours of a hill. Sometimes, a single or multi bank and ditch system is constructed across the top of the hill, as at Dorstone.

Revetment: stone wall (usually) designed to hold an earth rampart in place.

Ring Ditch: a circular 'doughnut' shaped monument, very similar in structure to a henge. Many have been discovered to be ploughed-out barrows. Several examples are found in west Herefordshire.

Romano-British: the native British peoples of the Roman period who showed signs of Roman cultural influence.

Severn-Cotswold Group: a group of Middle and Late Neolithic tombs that are located in and around the Severn Valley and on the

Cotswolds. Examples are also found in south and north Wales. There are possibly three Severn-Cotswold tombs in Herefordshire. These tombs hold more than one burial (unlike earlier Dolmens). For example, the tomb at Parc-la-Breos Cwm on the Gower Coast had at least twenty-four incomplete skeletons.

Standing Stones: also known as Monoliths, they are single stones of varying size. Possibly Late Neolithic, but more probably Bronze Age in date. Their use and reason is debatable—they have even been considered as scratching stones for cattle, but are most probably territorial or symbolic markers in the landscape.

Univallate Hillfort: a hillfort with defences consisting of a single bank and ditch. Most hillforts in Herefordshire are of this type.

Appendix 1

Guide to the Main Sites in Herefordshire

Name	Grid Ref		Site Type
Palaeolithic			
Ganarew: King Arthur's Cave	5458	1558	Cave
Ganarew: Merlin's Cave	5562	1533	Cave
Sarnesfield	38	49	Axe+Bl
Mesolithic			
Dorstone Hill	32	42	Flints
Fownhope: Nupend Farm	58	35	Flints
Ganarew: King Arthur's Cave	5458	1558	Flint Scr.
Kington: Arrow Court	27	54	Flints
Much Marcle: Gamage Farm	64	31	Flint Scr.
Peterchurch: Woodbury Hill	34	40	Flints
Vowchurch Common	36	37	Bl
Wellington Heath: Frith Farm	71	39	Flint Scr.
Neolithic			
Arthur's Stone	3189	4312	Ch.Tomb
Bach Long Barrow	2765	4287	Ch.Tomb
Buckton: Shed Field	38	74	Axe+Flints
Cefn Hill	27	38	Axe+Flints
Cross Lodge Long Barrow	3325	4168	Ch.Tomb
Dinedor Settlement	5350	3720	Settlement
Dorstone Settlement	3260	4230	Settlement
Dunseal Long Barrow	3913	3382	Ch.Tomb
Fownhope	57	33	Axe+Flints+A
Fownhope	57	36	Axe+Flints+P
Fownhope:Tump Farm	57	33	Axe+Flints+A
Ganarew: King Arthur's Cave	5458	1558	P+Flints
Ganarew: Merlin's Cave	5562	1533	P
Letton: Oakers Hill	34	46	Axe+Flints+A
Park Wood Chambered Tomb	3565	3347	Ch.Tomb
Peterchurch: Woodbury Hill 2	34	41	Axe+Flints
Whitney-on-Wye: Stowe Farm	2828	4771	Henge

Bronze Age

Aymestrey: Aymestrey Pit	42	66	Cist/P
Buckton Park	3959	7231	Round Barrow
Colwall	7679	4210	Round Barrow
Combe: Combe Meadow	3478	6348	Round Barrow
Craswall: Cefn Hill	276	383	Round Barrow
Dorstone	306	422	Standing Stone
Goodrich (Queen's Stone)	562	182	Standing Stone
King's Pyon	4425	4895	Round Barrow
Kinsham	3586	8641	Round Barrows
Kinsham	358	643	Standing Stone
Longtown	300	283	Cairn & Circle
Mathon	737	448	Cemetery
Michaelchurch	300	373	Standing Stone
Michaelchurch Escley	301	373	Round Barrow
Midsummer Hill	7621	3739	Round Barrow/P
Much Marcle: Gamage Farm	6505	3112	Settlement
Pembridge: Milton Cross	3825	6012	Round Barrow
Pembridge: Milton Cross	3850	6020	Cemetery
Pembridge: Milton Cross	3865	6028	Round Barrow
St Weonards	497	235	Standing Stone
Sutton (Wergin's Stone)	530	439	Standing Stone
Titley	3237	5868	Round Barrow
Walford: Walford Farm	3858	7233	Round Barrow

The Iron Age   Size,ha

Aconbury, Aconbury	7.0	504	330	Hillfort
Bach, Kimbolton	2.7	546	603	Hillfort
Brandon, Adforton	0.8	402	723	Hillfort
Capler, Woolhope	4.1	593	329	Hillfort
Cherryhill, Fownhope	2.2	577	352	Hillfort
Credenhill, Credenhill	20.0	450	446	Hillfort
Croft Ambrey, Aymestrey	9.1	445	688	Hillfort
Coxall Knoll, Buckton	3.3	366	734	Hillfort
Dinedor, Lower Bullingham	3.5	510	363	Hillfort
Dinmore, Hope-under-Dinmore	9.6	520	519	Hillfort
Dorstone Promontory Hillfort	0.2	325	422	Hillfort
Downton, Downton-on-the-Rock	0.2	429	732	Hillfort
Eaton, Eaton Bishop	7.3	453	393	Hillfort
Ethelbert's, Dormington	1.9	587	389	Hillfort
Gaer Cop, Hentland	6.8	537	253	Hillfort
Ganarew: Arthur's Cave		546	157	Cave
Ganarew: Merlin's Cave		556	153	Cave
Haffield, Donnington	1.9	723	339	Hillfort
Herefordshire Beacon	13.0	760	460	Hillfort
Ivington, Brierley	9.2	485	546	Hillfort
Kenchester: Field Barn Farm		446	426	Settlement
Little Doward, Ganarew	8.8	540	160	Hillfort
Midsummer Hill, Eastnor	7.6	760	374	Hillfort
Oldbury, Much Marcle	7.0	632	326	Hillfort
Pen Twyn, Brilley	0.8	238	486	Hillfort
Poston Hill, Vowchurch	1.6	359	377	Hillfort
Pyon Wood, Aymestrey	3.6	423	664	Hillfort
Risbury, Humber	11.0	541	553	Hillfort
Rowen Tree, Ross-on-Wye	8.8	603	225	Hillfort
Sutton Walls, Sutton	10.4	525	464	Hillfort
Wall Hills, Ledbury	3.6	630	598	Hillfort
Wall Hills, Thornbury	8.8	630	598	Hillfort
Walterstone, Walterstone	4.5	349	251	Hillfort
Wapley, Presteigne	6.0	346	625	Hillfort
Wellington Quarry, Leominster		508	480	Settlement

Questionable Sites

Neolithic

Clifford: Whitehouse Farm	2490	4628	R.D./Henge
Peterchurch: Woodbury Hill	3440	4140	Long Barrow

Neolithic/Bronze Age

Fownhope	5768	3606	Barrow
Holme Lacy: Holme Lacy Park	5510	3480	Barrow
Madley: Upper Chilstone House	3992	3927	Barrow/Henge
Whitney: Stowe Farm	2828	4771	R.D./Henge

Bronze Age

Adforton: Brandon	3998	7242	Round Barrow
Kinsham	3606	6396	Round Barrow
Leintwardine	4001	7621	Round Barrow
Leintwardine: the church	4050	7420	Round Barrow
Peterchurch: Common Bach	3074	4052	R.D./Henge
Peterchurch: Mowbatch Farm	3474	3918	Round Barrow
Titley: Flintsham Farm	3256	5882	Round Barrow
Winforton	2851	4625	Round Barrow
Yatton	437	669	Round Barrow

Iron Age

Garway: Cocksheath	4700	2080	Hillfort
Holme Lacy: Ramsden Coppice	5330	3480	Hillfort
Lingen	3700	6680	Hillfort
Weston-under-Penyard	64	25	Settlement
Willey: Hell Peak	3290	6670	Hillfort

Key

A	Arrowhead
Bl	Blade
Ch. Tomb	Chambered Tomb
Flint Scr.	Flint Scraper
P	Pottery

Appendix 2

Major Excavations in Herefordshire

Many of Herefordshire's archaeological sites have at one time or another been investigated either by excavation or as part of a survey

Date	Site	Director
1870-71	King Arthur's Cave, Ganarew	W.S. Symonds
from 1910	Mathon Bronze Age Cemetery	(various)
1924	Queen's Stone, Goodrich	A. Watkins
1924-25	Merlin's Cave, Ganarew	T.F. Hewer
1925	Capler Camp Iron Age Hillfort	G.H. Jack & A.G.K. Hayter
1926-27	King Arthur's Cave, Ganarew	H. Taylor
1932	Olchon Valley Cist Burials	G. Marshall
1932-37	Poston Iron Age Hillfort	G. Marshall
1933	Peterchurch Iron Age Mound	G. Marshall
from 1934	Golden Valley Survey	R.S. Gavin Robinson
from 1946	Cefn Hill Survey	R.S. Gavin Robinson
1948-51	Sutton Walls Iron Age Hillfort	K.M. Kenyon
1955-57	King Arthur's Cave, Ganarew	A.M. ApSimon
1958	Poston Iron Age Hillfort	I.E. Anthony
1958-60	Dorstone Hill Survey	W.R. Pye
1960-66	Croft Ambrey Iron Age Hillfort	S.C. Stanford
1963	Credenhill Iron Age Hillfort	S.C. Stanford
1965-70	Midsummer Hill Iron Age Hillfort	S.C. Stanford
1965-70	Dorstone Occupation Site	C. Houlder & W.R. Pye
1993	The Wye Valley Project	N. Barton *

* Also included are caves and rock shelters from Huntsham Hill

Bibliography

(Trans. WC stands for Transactions of the
Woolhope Naturalists' Field Club)

Anthony, I.E. *The Iron Age Camp at Poston, Herefordshire* The
    Woolhope Naturalist's Field Club, Hereford 1958

Barber, C. & Williams, J.G. *The Ancient Stones of Wales* Blorenge
    1989
Brown, A.E. *Records of surface finds made in Herefeordshire*
    Trans. WC Vol XXXVII, 1961 pp77-91
    Round Barrows in Herefordshire Trans WC Vol XL,
    1970 pp 315-17

Chitty, L.F. *Late Bronze Age Spearhead from the Great Doward,
    South Herefordshire* Trans WC Vol XXXIV, 1952
    pp 21-3
    *Stone Axe (He 46/c) and Flint Implements from
    Buckton, N.W. Herefordshire* Trans WC Vol
    XXXVIII, 1964 pp 153-5
Clarke, B.B. *A Geologist looks at King Arthur's Cave* Trans. WC
    Vol XXXIV, 1953 pp 76-83
Corcoran, J.X.W.P., Lynch, F., Powell, T.G.E. & Scott, J.G.
    *Megalithic Enquiries in the West of Britain: A
    Liverpool Symposium* Liverpool 1969
Crawford, O.G.S. *Long Barrows of the Cotswolds* Gloucester 1925

Gavin Robinson, R.S. *Flint workers and flint users in the Golden
    Valley* Trans. WC 1934 pp 54-63
    *The Pre-historic occupation of Cefn Hill,
    near Craswall* Trans. WC Vol XXXII,
    1946 pp 32-7
    *Notes on Bronze Age settlements on Abbey
    Farm, Craswall* Trans. WC Vol XXXIII,
    1950 pp 112-7

H&WCC *Herefordshire Countryside Treasures* 1981
　　　　Archaeology in South Herefordshire—The Rural West
　　　　1981
Hewer, T.F. *First Report on Excavations in the Wye Valley*
　　　　Proceedings of the University of Bristol
　　　　Spelaeological Society 2 1925 pp 147-161
　　　　Second Report on Excavations in the Wye Valley
　　　　Proceedings of the University of Bristol
　　　　Spelaeological Society 2 1925 pp 216-28

Jack, G.H. & Hayter, A.G.K. *Capler Camp* Trans. WC 1925 pp 83-8
Jenkins, R.J. *Flint artifacts and other material found in the Kington
　　　　area during 1956 and 1957* Trans. WC Vol XXXV,
　　　　1957 pp 320-7

Kenyon, K.M. *Excavations at Sutton Walls Camp, Herefordshire,
　　　　1948-50* Trans. WC Vol XXXIII, 1950 pp 148-55

Leather, E.M. *Folk-Lore of Herefordshire* Hereford 1970

Marshall, G. *Report on the discovery of two Bronze Age cists in the
　　　　Olchon Valley, Herefordshire* Trans. WC 1932 pp
　　　　147-53
　　　　*Lower Park Wood Camp. (?) Poston, In the parish of
　　　　Vowchurch, and some remarks on the Iron Age in
　　　　Herefordshire* Trans. WC 1933 pp 21-9
　　　　*Report on the excavation of a prehistoric mound in the
　　　　parish of Peterchurch, Herefordshire* Trans. WC
　　　　1933 pp 30-5

Norwood, J.F.L. *Prehistoric accessions to Hereford Museum* Trans.
　　　　WC Vol XXXV, 1961 pp 316-20
　　　　*Report from Hereford Museum. 1. Prehistoric
　　　　accessions to Hereford Museum* Trans. WC Vol
　　　　XXXVII, 1961 pp 103-7

Pye, W.R. *Report on Prehistoric Finds in North-west Herefordshire*
　　　　Trans. WC Vol XXXVI, 1958 pp 80-3

    A Discoidal Knife from Walford, Ross-on-Wye Trans.
        WC Vol XL, 1970 pp 312-4

Stanford, S.C. *Credenhill Camp, Herefordshire: An Iron Age*
        Hillfort Capital The Royal Archaeological
        Institute 1971
        Croft Ambrey (1960-1966) Woolhope Naturalists'
        Field Club pub., Hereford 1974
        The Archaeology of the Welsh Marches Second
        Edition 1991

Taylor, H. *King Arthur's Cave, Near Whitchurch, Ross-on-Wye*
        Proceedings of the University of Bristol Spelaeological
        Society 3 1958 pp 59-83

Watkins, A. *Report from sectional editors: Archaeology* Trans. WC
        Vol XIX, 1933 pp 41-7
Williams, J.G. *Herefordshire's Prehistoric Standing Stones* Trans.
        WC Vol XXXVIII, 1964 pp 255-6

Also from Logaston Press

The Folklore of Hereford & Worcester

by Roy Palmer. An up to date account covering places, people, churches, superstitions, the supernatural, witchcraft, work, song, stories, dance and the seasons. 288pp £8.95 ISBN 1 873827 02 4

Who killed Simon Dale? & other murder mysteries

by crime writer Kate Clarke. 14 true stories set in Herefordshire and the Welsh borders. Some cases are unsolved, in others doubt is cast on the verdict. 208pp £6.95 ISBN 1 873827 03 2

The Spirit of Herefordshire

by Jill Howard-Jones. Twenty-two Herefordshire characters tell their own stories, extrapolating from known facts, or occasionally from long believed folklore. Suitable for young and old alike, with numerous illustrations. 176pp £7.95 ISBN 1 873827 14 8

Walks & More

by Andrew Johnson & Stephen Punter. A walking and guide book covering central Wales, Herefordshire, Worcestershire west of the Severn and southern Shropshire. 80 circular walks, a gazetteer to over 150 towns, villages and places of interest, plus chapters on history, agriculture, folklore, cider, beer, art and literature. 336pp paperback, illustrations, maps. £7.95 ISBN 0 9510242 6 4

Walks in Southern Powys & the Borders

by Andrew Johnson, 35 walks in an area of stunning beauty. Notes on the history plus several illustrations. £4.95 ISBN 0 9510242 8 0

Alfred Watkins—A Herefordshire Man

by Ron Shoesmith, Hereford city's archaeologist. Watkins, the author of *The Old Straight Track* which gave birth to ley lines, had many other varied interests—including brewing, photography and steam cars. Includes 80 photographs, many by Watkins. £5.95 ISBN 0 9510242 7 2